Texas UFO Tales
from Denison 1878 to Stephenville 2008

Mike Cox & Renee Roderick

ISBN
1-933177-18-7 (10 digit)
978-1-933177-18-2 (13 digit)

Library of Congress Control Number: 2009937266

First Edition

Printed in the United States of America
Published by Atriad Press LLC
13820 Mcthuen Green
Dallas, TX 75240
(972) 671-0002
www.atriadpress.com

Cover photograph courtesy of NASA

Table of Contents

INTRODUCTION

I was a third grader in Dallas when a rash of UFO sightings around the South Plains town of Levelland made headlines in Big D and around the world. While not yet old enough to hang on every word of the newspaper coverage, I clearly remember the stir that incident and other reports of mysterious aerial lights or objects created in the mid-to-late 1950s.

I also distinctly recall seeing a newspaper photograph of a contraption some hoaxer built in an attempt to fool the public into thinking that an alien spacecraft had landed near Grapevine. While some people attributed the things they saw in the sky to government secrets or intelligent life from another world, others got their kicks doctoring photographs or creating "evidence" of space visitors.

In the spring of 1957, as I finished the second grade at the demonstration school at the Texas State College for Women in Denton (now Texas Women's University), I became a victim of a UFO prank myself. When my mother brought me home from school one day, the male college student who lived in the other side of our duplex came over to tell me he had picked up something on his shortwave radio that might interest me.

Likely sipping a cold Grapette soda, I went next door and stood in his living room as he fiddled with knobs and switches on one of several gray metal boxes that held tubes and coils and amplifiers. He reminded me of a somewhat younger

1

version of the brainy character on television's "Watch Mr. Wizard," the NBC series that ran from 1951 to 1965.

"Listen to what I picked up on my shortwave the other night," he said.

Our neighbor flipped a switch, and a reel-to-reel tape recorder started rolling.

At this late date, I won't try to recreate what the tape said, but it sounded like the last words of a spaceship commander about to crash. The alien pilot—who just happened to speak English with a Texas accent—shouted a Mayday-Mayday-Mayday, noted his position, and reported his craft was hurling out of control toward Planet Earth. Then, in midsentence, his voice cut off, his spaceship obviously having crashed and exploded. Who knows? The craft might have gone down near Denton.

Only nine, I believed every word of what I had heard—at least until Joe College and my mother started laughing and I realized I had been hornswaggled. Even so, I still wanted to believe I had heard a radio transmission from a flying saucer. In that era, with talk of atomic-powered spaceships and colonization of the moon and Mars by the 1970s, anything seemed possible.

That incident amounted to the closest encounter I had with the UFO waves of the 1950s, but flying saucers quickly became as much a part of American popular culture as poodle skirts and hula-hoops. No matter their origin—outer space or our collective imagination—UFOs spun into the mass media's solar system of newspapers, magazines, books, radio, television, and film.

The 1956 movie "Earth vs. the Flying Saucers" had held me on the edge of my seat, and Sheb Wooley's Top 40 song "Purple People Eater" became one of my favorite sing-along tunes. I used paper plates taped together to create my own fleet of flying saucers and fully expected that by the time I grew up I would be able to travel to space as casually as my mother drove to the grocery store.

Then the Eisenhower years faded into the turbulent-to-psychedelic 1960s. Other, bigger stories competed with UFO sightings for news coverage. From the assassination of a president to the summer of love to the Vietnam War, the decade expanded our minds and tarnished our hopeful idealism. Even the 1969 moon landing could not fully restore the flying saucer dreams of my generation's youth. And the Air Force's decision to stop officially investigating UFOs that same year made it harder for those still interested to keep track of sightings.

My personal gullibility was cured by nearly twenty years as a reporter, and another fifteen as a spokesman for the Texas Department of Public Safety. During both of those phases of my career, I followed news reports of the occasional UFO sightings in Texas, including some of the incidents covered in this book. When residents of Stephenville started seeing strange lights in the sky in early January 2008, I decided to see if I could come up with enough Texas UFO stories for a book. After a bit of research, I found plenty.

With several other pending book projects, I approached my friend, Renee Roderick, and asked if she would like to coauthor this one. An East Texas child of the space race era, Renee is married to a man born near Fort Worth during the well-publicized North Texas UFO wave of August 1965. To her, this explains a lot, not the least her husband's keen interest in the movie "Alien" and its many sequels.

Renee had a bit of a head start on this book in the form of an article she wrote about Roswell in 1999, as the media rehashed the events of the 20th century and the second millennium. Her files fortunately included notes from interviews with key UFO figures since deceased. Research for that article—and this book—gave her a deeper appreciation for the long-lasting effects of Cold War secrecy. As Dr. Edward Uhler Condon wrote in the final report of a government-sanctioned UFO research project in 1969, "Where secrecy is known to exist one can never be absolutely sure that he knows the complete truth."

The result of our collaboration is a book by two native Texans and former reporters who have spent most of our lives seeking the truth and trying to make it interesting. Striving for the journalistic objectivity we were trained in, we have tried to tell these stories down the middle, with neither hype nor hyperskepticism.

Renee and I are writers, not scientists, conspiracy theorists, or cosmic theologians. Neither of us believes in little green men (or women), but both of us believe that UFO stories—if nothing else—are fun to read. And fun to write, for that matter. Most of these stories are simply interpretive compilations of what amounts to modern folklore, but some do make us wonder. Although told from a Texas perspective, these tales also represent a microcosm of the American UFO experience.

As for Renee and I, we have no dog in the fight between confirmed skeptics and true believers. In a sense, UFOs have existed since humans first looked up into the sky. Some of greatest stories and scientific breakthroughs in history resulted from man's attempt to understand and explain what he saw there. We have just tried to tell a few UFO stories with a Texas twist. We also recognize that while the truth behind UFOs may be strange enough on its own, old-time Texas yarn spinners never let the truth get in the way of a good story. Imaginative scoundrels in the late 1800s proved that point by spinning fantastic tales about strange aerial machines and killer meteors.

In the end, it's hard to fathom that any sentient human being looking at the stars on a moonless night in far West Texas, hundreds of miles from any major cities, can believe Earth is the only place in the universe intelligent life exists. But as various government and scientific investigators have concluded over the years, no irrefutable evidence of extraterrestrial visitors has been found. Many others would argue that, by the same token, nothing has proven that flying saucers are merely figments of imagination or wishful thinking.

Mike Cox
Austin, Texas

5

U.S. Government UFO Investigation Timeline

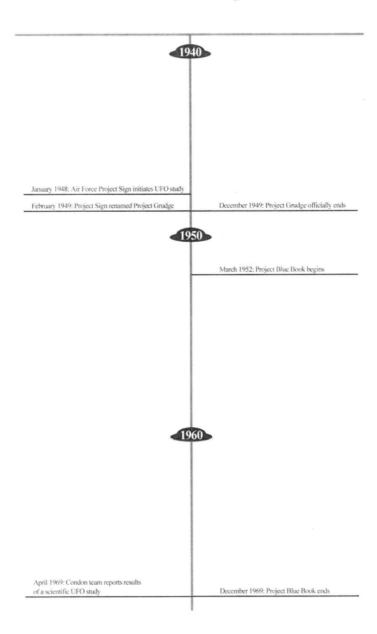

1940

January 1948: Air Force Project Sign initiates UFO study

February 1949: Project Sign renamed Project Grudge

December 1949: Project Grudge officially ends

1950

March 1952: Project Blue Book begins

1960

April 1969: Condon team reports results
of a scientific UFO study

December 1969: Project Blue Book ends

Texas UFO Timeline

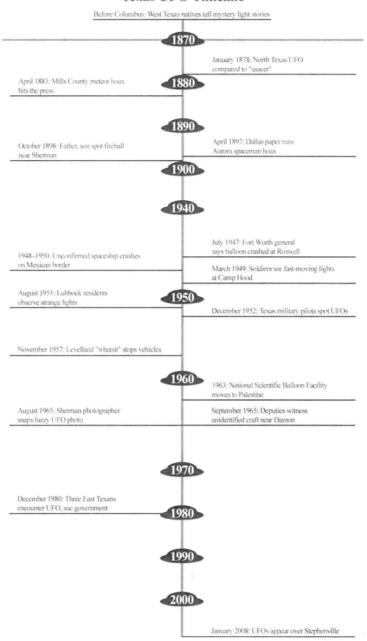

Before Columbus: West Texas natives tell mystery light stories

1870

January 1878: North Texas UFO compared to "saucer"

April 1883: Mills County meteor hoax hits the press

1880

1890

October 1898: Father, son spot fireball near Sherman

April 1897: Dallas paper runs Aurora spaceman hoax

1900

1940

July 1947: Fort Worth general says balloon crashed at Roswell

1948-1950: Unconfirmed spaceship crashes on Mexican border

March 1949: Soldiers see fast-moving lights at Camp Hood

August 1951: Lubbock residents observe strange lights

1950

December 1952: Texas military pilots spot UFOs

November 1957: Levelland "whatsit" stops vehicles

1960

1963: National Scientific Balloon Facility moves to Palestine

August 1965: Sherman photographer snaps fuzzy UFO photo

September 1965: Deputies witness unidentified craft near Damon

1970

December 1980: Three East Texans encounter UFO, sue government

1980

1990

2000

January 2008: UFOs appear over Stephenville

CHAPTER 1:
IN THE BEGINNING:
TEXAS' EARLIEST UFOS

Considering all the states of the Union, Texas' pedigree does not extend all that far back, especially compared with the northeastern states, but when it comes to UFOs the Lone Star State has a unique claim: The first ever usage of the word "saucer" to describe a UFO occurred in Texas.

Denison was a bustling railroad town when farmer reported "saucer"

It happened in 1878, near the Grayson County city of Denison, then a booming North Texas railroad town. The sighting made page-one news in the January 25, 1878, edition of the long-defunct Denison *Daily News.* Here's the complete story:

A Strange Phenomenon

From Mr. John Martin, a farmer who lives some six miles north of this city, we learn the following strange story: Tuesday morning [Jan. 22] while out hunting, his attention was directed to a dark object high up in the southern sky. The peculiar shape and velocity with which the object seemed to approach riveted his attention and he strained his eyes to discover its character.

When first noticed, it appeared to be about the size of an orange, which continued to grow in size. After gazing at it for some time Mr. Martin became blind from long looking and left off viewing it for a time in order to rest his eyes. On resuming his view, the object was almost overhead and had increased considerably in size, and appeared to be going through space at wonderful speed.

When directly over him it was about the size of a large saucer and was evidently at great height. Mr. Martin thought it resembled, as well as he could judge, a balloon. It went as rapidly as it had come and was soon lost to sight in the heavenly skies. Mr. Martin is a gentleman of undoubted veracity and this strange occurrence, if it was not a balloon, deserves the attention of our scientists.

A close reading of this 210-word story makes it clear that Martin did not say he saw a flying saucer, but an object "about the size of a large saucer." Too, the newspaper piece makes no inference that the object came from another world. In fact, Martin "thought it resembled…a balloon."

But at some point, someone ran onto this story and inducted it into UFO lore.

An even more careful review of the facts surrounding this 1878 story reveals the distinct possibility of a long-ago misunderstanding on someone's part: It appears the UFO sighting occurred near Dallas, not Denison. True, the story ran in the Denison newspaper, but according to a retrospective article published by the Dallas *Morning News* during the North Texas UFO flap of August 1965, the Denison newspaper merely reprinted a report that first appeared in a Dallas newspaper. According to the *Morning News* article, the saucer story in the Denison newspaper "recounts a piece that appeared in the old Dallas *Herald*." Dallas' first daily, the *Herald* came out every morning except Monday.

If that is correct, Martin had a farm in Dallas County, not near Denison. At least both towns have names starting with a "D." And back then, the two places were about the same size.

The 1880 U.S. Census shows no farmers named Martin living in Dallas County, but enumerators found three John Martins living in Collin County, just to the north of Dallas. All made their living as farmers. To even further muddy the water, the same census also lists a tenant farmer named John E. Martin living in Grayson County.

Whichever John Martin saw the saucer-sized object, and wherever the story first appeared, it did not create much of a splash downstate. The Austin *Daily Statesman*, then an afternoon sheet in the capital city, was silent on the reported event in the North Texas skies. Neither is there any easily findable evidence that the tale received national or international notice in the press, unlike subsequent aerial sightings.

While the Dallas-or-Denison sighting is apparently the first time anyone ever compared an unidentified airborne object to being the size of a saucer, the UFO report was not the first in Texas. That distinction, at least according to Donald Keyhoe, a former Marine aviator turned writer, belongs to Bonham.

In 1949, *True*, then one of the nation's leading men's magazines, assigned Keyhoe to do a story on flying saucers. His research made him a believer that many UFOs were indeed alien spacecraft, and his January 1950 article is largely credited with triggering the UFO phenomenon in popular culture. Later that year, expanding on his *True* research, he wrote a book that became a best seller, *The Flying Saucers Are Real.*

As he describes in chapter seven, Keyhoe was sitting in the lounge of a DC-6 airliner flying from New York to Washington when he began perusing a copy of the report issued by Project Sign, the Air Force's first study of the UFO phenomenon. The document contained summaries of various early articles detailing mysterious aerial sightings long before the term UFO had been coined. Most of the reports were from other countries, but the major found a few with references to unusual events in the United States in the final third of the 19th century.

An incident at Bonham in the summer of 1873 (Keyhoe did not give the month or day) was one of the first reports of an unknown aerial object in the United States and the first known sighting in Texas.

He wrote:

> It was broad daylight when a strange, fast-moving object appeared in the sky, southwest of the town. For a moment, the people of Bonham stared at the thing, not believing their eyes. The only flying device then known was the drifting balloon. But this thing was tremendous, and speeding so fast its outlines were almost a blur.
>
> Terrified farmers dived under their wagons. Townspeople fled indoors. Only a few hardy souls remained in the streets. The mysterious object circled Bonham twice, then raced off to the east and vanished. Descriptions of the strange machine varied from round or oval to cigar- shaped....
>
> Twenty-four hours after the Bonham incident, a device of the same description appeared at Fort Scott, Kansas. Panic-stricken soldiers fled the parade ground as the thing flashed overhead. In a few seconds it disappeared, circling toward the north.

Though Keyhoe wrote that Frank Edwards, a Mutual Broadcasting System newsman who also did freelance writing, "investigated this case" and provided him details, he did not offer further specifics in his book.

Air Force researchers apparently had gotten their information from a front-page story in the New York *Times* of July 6, 1873. The *Times* article was a partial reprinting of a report first published in the Bonham *Enterprise*, though the New York newspaper did not give the date. Only 115 words long, the piece read:

> The very worst case of delirium tremens on record is one told by the Bonham (Texas) *Enterprise*, which says that a few days ago a man residing five or six miles from that place "saw something resembling an enormous serpent floating in a cloud that was passing over his farm. Several parties of men and boys, at work in the fields, observed the same thing, and were seriously frightened. It seemed to be as large and long as a telegraph pole, was of a yellow striped color, and seemed to float along without any effort. They could see it coil itself up, turn over, and thrust forward its huge head as if striking at something."

Though the story made news in Bonham and got picked up by the New York *Times*, newspapers in Texas seemed to have ignored the report. The Galveston *News*, then the state's newspaper of record, did not enlighten its readers with the tale of the flying serpent.

Eighteen years later, in June 1891, another report of a mysterious airborne object over North Texas appeared in the

Dublin *Progress*. Though the headline read "Meteoric Explosion," those who read deeper into the story found a startling claim.

"Quite a little excitement was created last Saturday night by the bursting of what is supposed by those who were present to have been a meteor, near Wasson & Miller's gin," the article began. Sticking with his opening qualifier, the reporter continued, "Quite a number witnessed the explosion and nearly everyone in that portion of the city heard the report eminating [sic] therefrom, which is said to have sounded somewhat like the report of a bomb-shell."

The principal witness, described as "a gentleman who usually tells the truth" who had not spoken "with a view to…publication" said he first saw the meteor when it was about 300 feet in the air over Erath County. The man said the object "bore a striking resemblance to a bale of cotton suspended in the air after having been saturated in kerosene oil and ignited, except that it created a much brighter light, almost dazzling those who perceived it."

While the man had been badly frightened by what he saw, his reluctance to speak on the record, or go into too much more detail, apparently had more to do with what he had been doing at the time of the sighting rather than the event itself. "We are convinced from his statements that his position at the time must have been very embarrassing and that very little time was spent in scientific investigations," the journalist went on, leaving to his readers to imagine what the witness might have been up to on a Saturday night that he did not want the rest of the community to know about.

On the Sabbath, the witness arose a calmer and perhaps more sober man. Returning to the scene of the aerial explosion, he found "the weeds, grass, bushes and vegetation of every description for many yards burned to a crisp, also discovering a number of peculiar stones and pieces of metal, all of a leaden color…."

Though burnt grass and scattered remnants could be evidence of a meteorite's impact, the man said he found something entirely out of place: "Small fragments of manuscript and a scrap, supposed to be part of a newspaper, but the language in both was entirely foreign to him, and, in fact, no one has yet been found who has ever seen such a language before, hence no information could be gained from their examination."

The story makes no inference that the torn documents printed in some unknown language could have anything to do with the crash of an intelligently controlled craft of some sort, but a scattering of shredded paper amid the other debris certainly posed a sharp contrast to the other reported evidence.

The newspaper writer concluded:

> At this juncture your reporter requested that he be shown these wonderful fragments of such a miraculous whole, but the narrator had worked himself up to such a pitch of excitement that it was impossible to get him to grasp the significance of our request, and [we] were compelled to leave him a victim to his own bewildered fancy and to ruminate the seemingly miraculous story he has just related. Thus was a reportorial zealot denied the boon of seeing fragments of the most remarkable substance ever known to explode near Wasson & Miller's gin.

The next early-day aerial oddity also occurred in North Texas.

Keyhoe wrote:

> A strange shadow was noted on the clouds at Fort Worth, Texas, on April 8, 1913. It appeared to be caused by some large body hovering motionless above the clouds. As the cloud layer moved, the shadow remained in the same position. Then it changed size, diminishing, and quickly disappeared, as if it had risen vertically. A report on this was given in the Weather Bureau Review of that year, Number 4-599.

Judging by the relatively low-key newspaper coverage of these events, Texans in the 19th century and early 20th century seemed content to accept unexplained phenomenon as just that. In time, Texans and others across the nation would start asking more questions when strange things happened.

CHAPTER 2:
DEATH FROM OUTER SPACE:
OR JOE MULHATTON STRIKES AGAIN

The telegraphic news flashed across America and the world like a shooting star—a huge meteorite had hit near the heart of Texas, falling with devastating effect in Brown County.

"A great meteor fell near Williams Ranch at 2 o'clock Sunday morning," the *Daily News* in Newport, Rhode Island, reported on Monday April 16, 1883. The giant object from the heavens had a hellish impact, "killing several head of cattle and destroying the dwelling of Martinez Garcia, a Mexican herdsman, who with his wife and five children were burned in the ruins."

The report went on to describe the meteor as "a massive ball of fire" that created an earthquake-like shock as it embedded itself "nearly a hundred feet in the ground."

The force of the impact, the 139-word news item continued, shattered nearly every window in the community of Williams Ranch (now in present-day Mills County, cut from Brown County in 1887), tossing people from their beds, tumbling merchandise from store shelves and collapsing several buildings. Afterward, "the air was filled with sulphurous gas."

Readers of a dispatch published in New York City learned that the giant object from space that landed in Texas "is still steaming and covers an acre of ground."

A few days later, the April 20 issue of *The Forest News* in Jackson County, Georgia, amplified on the startling news from Central Texas: The Garcia family (no first names given) had not been burned in the ruins, but buried in the ruins. Whether they were dead or alive was not mentioned.

"This is the largest meteor that has ever fallen and it has already been visited by many people and doubtless will continue to attract great attention for months to come," the Georgia newspaper went on. "It has occasioned great excitement not only here but in all [of] the surrounding county." Indeed, another newspaper reported "thousands are visiting the scene."

In the Midwest, the Burlington, Iowa, *Weekly Hawkeye* of April 26 featured a story about the Williams Ranch incident headlined "A Visitor From the Skies." While Williams Ranch "is a place not mentioned in ordinary geography," the piece began, "it has just succeeded in becoming suddenly notorious."

Indeed, Williams Ranch could not claim to be one of Texas' more populated or better-known places. The town, which had 250 or so residents, got its name from John Williams, a rancher who settled in the area in 1855. The community had grown up near a spring in the middle of Williams' holdings. Since the average horseback rider could only travel thirty or so miles a day, and a wagon or stage coach less than that, Williams Ranch became a stopping point for the stage line that connected Austin to Brownwood and developed into a trade center for surrounding ranches. The town had a store, a mill, a school, a hotel called The Florida, a post office opened in 1877, telegraph service, and a cemetery.

Assuming anyone could ever get to their bodies, that small graveyard was where the victims of the tragedy would be laid to rest. The "colossal meteor" had driven the poor Garcia family some one hundred feet underground, according to another newspaper report. Seventy feet of the space rock extended above ground. One report said the protruding alien mass looked something like the red sandstone Tarrant County courthouse in Fort Worth. Looking on the bright side of things, the article noted that as soon as the object cooled off, it could be fenced in and "shown as a natural curiosity." The fall of the "monster," the report continued, had naturally created considerable excitement in the area.

The Iowa newspaper then offered its subscribers a lesson in astronomy: "It is generally believed meteors are associated with comets. They may be fragments of disrupted comets....If these small bodies occasionally reach the earth there is no reason why comets themselves should not strike us. After all, a meteoric stone only an inch in diameter differs from the largest planetary body only in size."

Joe Mulhatton

The Williams Ranch meteor strike was not the only astronomical phenomena in the news that year. Only twelve days before the Texas incident sparked along the wires, the April 5, 1883, edition of the Decatur *Daily Republic* informed its readers that a large meteorite had splashed into Muskegon Lake in Illinois. Interestingly, it, too, left the odor of sulfur in the air.

The 1883 news coverage of the reported Williams Ranch incident must have seemed far-fetched, but meteors do fall to earth. When that happens, they are called meteorites. (In the 19th century, the more common term was aerolites.) Less common is a meteorite actually hitting something other than just the ground or water.

A Web site that records confirmed accounts of meteorites striking manmade objects, humans, or animals lists only 101 such incidents worldwide since 1790. Of those, two occurred in the Lone Star state. The first happened on September 9, 1961, when a meteorite crashed into a building at Bells, a North Texas community in Grayson County. The second confirmed strike happened March 22, 1998, when a small meteorite pinged a street in Monahans, in West Texas.

Interestingly, the Web site makes no mention of the spectacular 1883 impact in Mills County. That's because it never happened.

The Galveston *Daily News*, back then Texas' newspaper of record, had reported as early as April 17 that "no meteor has fallen at Williams Ranch.... The report is false." The same day, a St. Louis newspaper said a "reliable gentlemen" from Fort Worth had wired the Associated Press to inform the national news cooperative that the Williams Ranch story was not true. The man from Fort Worth went further: "The story...is one of Joe Mulhatton's lies. Mulhatton is the man who sold the Mammoth cave to be shipped to England."

Whoever sent that telegram was correct. The Williams Ranch meteor strike occurred only in the fertile if often-pickled brain of one of 19th century America's more fascinating if little-known characters.

The son of a Presbyterian minister, Mulhatton was born near Pittsburgh, Pennsylvania, in 1853. After receiving a public school education, Mulhatton took up the drummer's trade, as it was then called. He traveled the nation peddling a variety of products and seems to have enjoyed considerable success in business. At twenty-five, he moved to Kentucky to sell blue jeans for a Blue Grass State manufacturer.

In addition to being a good salesman, Mulhatton had developed a hobby he called "novelistic journalism." Put in plainer language, he dreamed up wildly imaginative hoaxes and planted stories about them in newspapers.

"I cannot remember the first lie I ever told," he later wrote.

One of Mulhatton's earliest hoaxes, a story claiming that George Washington's body had petrified and would be put on public display, appeared in 1877. A year later, in his new Kentucky home, he penned a story about the discovery of a twenty-three-mile-long cavern and the underground river that flowed through it. He said someone already was at work building a riverboat to take excursionists up and down the subterranean stream that traversed the Grand Crystal Cave. Among the attractions would be numerous petrified remains found in the enormous cavern. Topping that tale a couple of years later, Mulhatton wrote a report that a young girl who had tied one too many balloons to her waist had become airborne and drifted away to the horror of her family and friends.

The preacher's kid from the Keystone State clearly got a charge from pulling the proverbial wool over the heads of gullible newspaper editors and their readers. He also found much amusement, and possibly inspiration, in the bottle.

"Although my life has been at least as merry as that of the average member of my profession, it has been by no means an easy one," he later admitted. Indeed, his penchant for strong drink eventually developed into chronic alcoholism.

Far too creative a liar to repeat himself, Mulhatton went on to numerous other hoaxes. Still, those of lesser imagination continued to report their own versions of the old sky-is-falling story.

"There seems to be some person in the associated press who makes it his business or pastime to invent aerolite discoveries," ranted a letter writer identified only by the initials W.E.H. in the Statesville, North Carolina, *Landmark* on June 24, 1886. "The first instance I can now recall was the alleged fall near Fort Worth, Texas, of an aerolite a mile in width. (The Williams Ranch stories all had a Fort Worth dateline.) When I read the press dispatch I telegraphed to Fort Worth and ascertained that the statement was a lie out of the whole cloth."

The letter-to-the-editor went on to describe three other recent aerolite hoaxes, concluding, "These canards have cost some expense for correspondence and telegraphy, and the fiend should be killed."

In 1890, Mulhatton publicly admitted his Williams Ranch hoax. On July 15 that year, the Galveston *Daily News* carried a story reprinted from the Kansas City *Times* headlined "The Original Mulhatton Talks: Of Course Nobody Believes Him, but Here Is What He Said."

Granting an audience to the KC reporter in one of that city's saloons, Mulhatton gave his version of the Williams Ranch story.

"I was talking to Bill Eads, a Louisville newspaperman...and he asked me to write him a story," Mulhatton said. "I told him I was out of ideas and couldn't do it. Just at that minute a little meteor shot across the blue dome of heaven, and it brought me an idea."

The inveterate hoaxer also may have read newspaper stories on the popular lantern-and-slide lectures of Princeton astronomy professor Charles A. Young (1834-1908). On January 30, 1883, the professor had addressed a large audience in New York City on meteors and comets. The New York

Times summarized Young's presentation on January 31, and other newspapers across the nation, in the style of the day, reprinted the piece. While Young had not said that a meteor impact could be catastrophic, he did note that the falling of meteors "is accompanied by loud explosions." As to their size, the scientist said Amherst College held a meteorite that weighed 450 pounds.

So Mulhatton told Eads he would write a story about a meteor. "I turned right around and got to work," he continued. "While Bill was talking to me of the newspaper business and the scoop he missed I wrote the story. I located the thing in Brown county, at Williams' Ranch near Brownwood, and worked in a lot of stuff about the fleeing populous and sulphurous smell that pervaded the atmosphere for miles. I said that the meteor sizzed and sizzled in the damp ground and withered plantations [sic] for acres and acres around, parching the ground into fire brick for many miles."

How he had ever heard of Williams Ranch and why he selected it as ground zero for his hoax, Mulhatton did not explain. Since Williams Ranch was a stopping place for almost anyone headed to Northwest Texas, it may be that at some point in peddling his products the hoaxer found himself in what was then Brown County.

Mulhatton continued his confession:

"Well, the story appeared in good season and the Associated Press sent the item out. In a week there were more scientists and newspapermen on their way to Texas than boarding houses of the state could accommodate. Some of them got lost in the mesquite brush and fed on the beans for weeks, and some of them got discouraged looking for the meteor and bought a hundred acres of five cent land and are living there yet, raising mosquitoes, tarantulas and children. I think it was the best thing for them that ever happened."

By 1884, a year after the Williams Ranch meteor hoax, Mulhatton had become so popular with his fellow traveling men that they "nominated" him for President at their annual meeting. With his name for once associated with a news story that was not a hoax, Mulhatton accepted the nomination and adopted a probusiness campaign platform. Despite his penchant for booze, he even favored prohibition.

One-time Comanche *Chief* editor Sidney J. Thomas later told his version of the Williams Ranch meteor story in his now-rare book, *Scrapbook*, a self-published collection of musings he brought out in the early 1900s.

In his telling, Thomas cast Mulhatton not as a drummer but as a reporter for an Eastern newspaper who happened to pass through Williams Ranch while traveling between Austin and Fort Worth. A group of rowdy cowboys, spotting a fancy-dressed greenhorn arriving on the stage, took him in charge at gunpoint and made him dance to the tune of exploding .45s.

"He was then," Thomas wrote, "forced to drink an overdose of tangle-foot, and while under its influence to write for his paper some startling imaginary occurrence that would attract attention to Williams Ranch." However, most references to Mulhatton indicate that true to his Irish heritage, no one would have had to force him to consume an intoxicating beverage.

According to Thomas, the "ruffians" held Mulhatton captive "pending the determination (of) the effect of the dispatch...on the world. The document was promptly published and a great sensation instantly produced...Scientists hurried to the scene to investigate the phenomenon, only to find the whole story a canard."

The 1883 incident, Thomas concluded, gave rise to a popular Mills County expression that endured for a generation: To "lie like a Mulhatton" meant prevarication "in the superlative degree." In fact, Mulhatton stood for years as a synonym for lie.

As for Mulhatton, broken down by years of hard drinking, he died in Arizona in 1913 or 1914—the exact date has not been determined.

While the great Williams Ranch meteor had existed only in the boozy imagination of Joe Mulhatton, he never knew that Texas actually had been blasted by a giant meteor that would have caused far more damage than he made up in his fanciful 1883 report.

Some 25,000 years ago, give or take a few, a 300-ton meteor burning through the atmosphere at some 27,000 miles an hour—10,000 miles an hour faster than the space shuttle travels when orbiting Earth—crashed to earth seven miles southwest of what is now Odessa. More than thirty feet in diameter, the supersonic visitor from space hit prehistoric West Texas, then a lush swampland, only a glancing blow. Part of the object broke off and imbedded itself into the limestone bedrock, and part of it shattered and scattered around the crater the impact created, but the bulk of it careened back into space like a giant glowing ping pong ball.

Even so, scientists believe the force of the impact exceeded the combined energy released by the explosions of the atomic bombs at Hiroshima and Nagasaki. For miles around, no living thing would have survived. Had anyone been around to see it from a safe distance, once the dirt and debris settled to earth, a crater 175 yards wide and thirty-three yards deep had been created.

While early residents of Ector County realized something had made a mighty big hole in the ground in their part of Texas, for years they thought a terrific gas blow out had caused the crater. Not until well into the 20th century did the scientific community finally come to realize that a large meteor had created the depression. The chain of events leading to that understanding began in 1920, when a local rancher found a baseball-sized chunk of metallic rock at the site. He gave the rock to Odessa mayor R.S. McKinney, who used it as a paperweight. When a visiting oilfield geologist happened to see it on McKinney's desk, he asked if he could send it to the U.S. Museum of Natural History for analysis. The mayor readily agreed, and the analysis showed the rock was a meteorite.

Aerial image of the Odessa meteor crater

In 1922, the geologist wrote an article for the *American Journal of Science*, suggesting that the depression in Ector County had not been caused by a gas explosion but by a meteor strike. Over the years, the crater has been the subject of ever more sophisticated scientific study. Scientists eventually discovered the crater is the larger of five sites in the immediate area, all caused by the glancing impact of the same object.

Today the Odessa meteor crater is a registered National Natural Landmark and open for self-guided tours. Two hundred and fifty miles to the east of Odessa, the scene of Texas' giant meteor hoax is a ghost town with only a cemetery as evidence it ever existed.

CHAPTER 3:
JUDGE PROCTOR'S WINDMILL:
THE AURORA SPACEMAN

When thorough readers of the Dallas *Morning News* got to page five that Monday morning, April 19, 1897, they saw a small headline that read: "A Windmill Demolishes It." Those four words did not amount to a particularly compelling journalistic come-on for the 283-word dispatch that appeared beneath it:

> Aurora, Wise Co., Tex., April 17. – (To The News) – About 6 o'clock this morning the early risers of Aurora were astonished at the sudden appearance of the airship which has been sailing through the country.
>
> It was traveling due north, and much nearer the earth than ever before. Evidently some of the machinery was out of order, for it was making a speed of only ten or twelve miles an hour and gradually settling toward the earth. It sailed directly over the

public square, and when it reached the north part of town collided with the tower of Judge Proctor's windmill and went to pieces with a terrific explosion, scattering debris over several acres of ground, wrecking the windmill and water tank and destroying the judge's flower garden.

The pilot of the ship is supposed to have been the only one on board, and while his remains are badly disfigured, enough of the original has been picked up to show that he was not an inhabitant of this world.

Mr. T.J. Weems, the United States signal service officer at this place and an authority on astronomy, gave it as his opinion that he was a native of the planet Mars.

Papers found on his person – evidently the record of his travels – are written in some unknown hieroglyphics, and can not be deciphered.

The ship was too badly wrecked to form any conclusion as to its construction or motive power. It was built of an unknown metal, resembling somewhat a mixture of aluminum

and silver, and it must have
weighed several tons.
The town is full of people
to-day who are viewing the
wreck and gathering specimens
of the strange metal from the
debris. The pilots [sic] funeral
will take place at noon to-
morrow.
– S.E. Haydon

The same story appeared in the Fort Worth *Register*, with
the exception of this new concluding sentence: "The pilot, who
was not an inhabitant of this world, was given a Christian
burial in the Aurora Cemetery." The story also omitted the
paragraph about the hieroglyphic ship's log. But the news
coverage ended with the Dallas and Fort Worth stories. The
Wise County *Messenger* made no mention of the purported
crash. Entering "Aurora" and "1897" into a searchable
newspaper archive Web site shows that the story appeared in
no other major newspaper anywhere in the United States.

No matter the intriguing content of the Wise County
dispatch, no one in 1897 took the story seriously. At the near
height of the Yellow Journalism era, newspaper editors did not
trouble themselves overmuch with ethical concerns, at least in
comparison to modern times. Back then, fiction in the guise of
news, from manufactured quotes to outright hoaxes, was as
common as patent medicine ads.

In fact, the Aurora story was one of hundreds of stories
reporting "airship" sightings that spread from west to east
across half the nation in 1896-1897, eventually including
eighteen states. The wave began November 17, 1896, when
dozens of people reported seeing a strange light above
Sacramento, California. Others said the light emanated from an
object—a cigar-shaped aerial craft. Newspapers

sensationalized the story, creating a virtual nuclear chain reaction of ever-stranger sightings reported in the public print.

The first reported sighting in the Lone Star State came on April 12, 1897, when two Ennis men said they saw an unknown aerial object silhouetted against the moon. Throughout the rest of the month, Texans from Childress to Beaumont and from Uvalde to Texarkana claimed to have seen strange things in the sky. In some instances, witnesses reported interacting with airship pilots and crewmembers. Circumstances and descriptions varied, but the general tone of the stories was that secretive inventors were experimenting with nonballoon machines that could not only fly, but travel long distances at significant speeds. What made the Aurora story different is that its author reported that the thing that crashed into Judge Proctor's windmill came from another world.

The reported sightings peaked that April. Less than a year later, the Spanish-American War broke out following the explosion of the Battleship Maine in Havana harbor on February 15, 1898. By that time, accounts of mysterious airships had disappeared from the media, replaced by stories of Admiral Dewey's warships and Teddy Roosevelt's Rough Riders. Soon America and the rest of the world entered the 20th century, eventually enduring a world war, the Great Depression, another world war, and the onset of a cold war. For more than sixty-nine years, the Aurora story remained dormant.

Then, in January 1967, Dallas *Morning News* columnist Frank X. Tolbert opened the day's stack of mail generated by his popular column, "Tolbert's Texas." One letter came from a reader enclosing a copy of an old newspaper story, Haydon's account of the Aurora airship crash.

Tolbert knew a good tale when he saw one, even if the guy on the copy desk who wrote the headline for his next column did not: "Did Plane Crash in Texas in 1897?" appeared in Big D's morning newspaper on January 4, 1967. Substituting

31

"Spaceship" for "Plane" would have been much catchier, but even so, the story of the Aurora spaceman had reentered Earth's orbit.

Telling the story in a tight dozen paragraphs, Tolbert promised his readers: "The next time I'm in Aurora I'm going to make some inquiries about that alleged funeral of the out-of-this-world pilot."

The long-time Dallas journalist, who fought in World War II as a Marine, would not know it for years, but he had already been scooped in his own back yard. The year before, an "investigator" for a British publication called *The Flying Saucer Review* had come to Texas to look into the Aurora story. His story appeared in that magazine's January-February issue before the Dallas *Morning News* piece hit the streets that winter. Also in 1966, Dr. Alfred E. Kraus of the Kilgore Research Institute at West Texas State University in Canyon had quietly looked into the Aurora story on behalf of the Condon Committee, an Air Force-funded investigation into UFOs being conducted by the University of Colorado under the direction of Dr. Edward Condon. Kraus talked with surviving Aurora old-timers, searched the purported crash site with a metal detector and reported to Condon that there was nothing to the story.

Tolbert finally got around to his Aurora follow-up in June 1968, but it was not much of one. Clearly, the columnist viewed the Aurora matter as just another quirky incident from Texas' past, a piece of 19th century fiction dressed up as a news story.

Still, it was an intriguing story, ripe for further journalistic exploitation. The Dallas *Times-Herald*'s Bill Case became the next Dallas journalist to stake out the Aurora tale. He not only immersed himself in the subject, he became part of the story. Case, a long-time Chicago-based Hearst reporter with all the well-honed instinct for a sensational story that background would imply, had been hired near the end of his career by the

Dallas afternoon newspaper. His beat was aviation, a field that included everything from aerospace to the relatively new Dallas-Fort Worth International Airport.

In a story appearing on March 25, 1973, Case reported that a team of "ufologists" led by Hayden Hewes of the Oklahoma City-based International UFO Bureau was "combing a cemetery in the ghost town of Aurora in Wise County for the grave of a UFO pilot reportedly buried there after his spaceship collided with a windmill and exploded April 19 [sic], 1897."

Historical marker in Aurora Cemetery

Though no tombstone in the cemetery bore the inscription "Unknown Martian," interest centered on a grave beneath the bent elbow-shaped limb of a large oak. The only thing indicating a burial was a rock bearing an unusual design, a horizontal delta with three small circles in it.

After visiting Aurora and talking with a few of its 200 or so residents, Case weighed in with another story on March 28. The reporter had interviewed 65-year-old Brawley Oates, an Aurora native who since 1945 had lived on the land where the crash reportedly occurred, Judge Proctor's old place.

"I've heard the story all my life," he told Case. "Of course, I'm not sure this was a UFO. But I believe something of this kind exists. There are too many similar reports from too many places to be coincidental."

While no windmill stood on the property in 1973, Oates figured it would have been near the place's old well. When its water went bad, he had covered it with a concrete slab and had another well drilled. However, some old-timers claimed Proctor never had a windmill on his place.

Case's biggest-yet Aurora story appeared on the front of the *Times-Herald*'s metropolitan page on May 17, 1973: "Metal unearthed may be UFO." The piece went on to report that Frank N. Kelley of Corpus Christi, a "scientific Texas treasure hunter" had found metal at the purported spaceship crash site the likes of which he had never seen.

"The fragments I recovered are small, thin and jagged as if torn apart by an explosion," Kelley said. "They look something like modern aircraft covering. But they are not aluminum, tin, iron, steel or any alloy I know. This metal looks so different I honestly don't know what it is."

The mystery metal, he continued, bounced back the same type of signal he got when waving his metal detector over the unmarked grave believed to contain the remains of the victim of the crash.

"The only explanation I can give for getting the same signals at the windmill site and in the grave more than a mile away is that the pilot whose body was torn apart was buried wearing some type of metal uniform or equipment which gives us the same reaction," Kelley told Case.

Kelley had used what Case called a "deep probe" metal detector on the hilltop where the windmill reportedly had stood as well as at the Aurora Cemetery. H.R. Idell, Aurora's town marshal, and Case accompanied Kelley as he combed the two sites.

"The most amazing aspect I see," Kelley went on, "is that most soil 20 to 30 feet around the former windmill...also gives off a somewhat less but almost identical electronic response even when there is no metal in it."

The pipe-smoking treasure hunter said he found more than a dozen pieces of metal, ranging from two to fourteen inches under ground.

With publication of this story, the Aurora investigation took off in the national media like a National Aeronautics and Space Administration (NASA) booster rocket. The Associated Press rewrote Case's article and distributed it nationally. Not to be outdone, rival wire service United Press International ran with the story as well. Other newspaper headlines writers exercised less objective caution than the *Times-Herald* had. The Odessa *American*, for one, ran a headline declaring: "Metal Recovered From Flying Object."

At least from the perspective of Hewes and Case, the next logical step needed to be opening the grave in question.

"We hope by exhuming the body we may obtain some of the same type of unusual metal from either his [the supposed space alien's] clothing or bones that was unearthed at the well site when we checked it with metal detectors," Hewes said.

Prior to this point, the small Wise County community had been cooperative with UFO investigators and reporters, though the Oakes had shut off access to their property except for the nonofficial "official" investigators. But the Aurora Cemetery dated back to 1861 and many of the ancestors of local residents lay buried there. Immediately after Hewes' pronouncement that the mystery grave needed to be dug up, the Aurora Cemetery

Association filed a petition in state district court seeking an injunction barring any grave openings in the cemetery.

Case, meanwhile, had found two places willing to analyze the metal found around the well. They agreed to do the work pro bono with one proviso: Their names had to be kept out of it. The reporter believed that if the metal analysis proved interesting, the chance of getting a judge to approve an exhumation order would be bolstered.

Continuing his efforts to shape the story, Case had been in contact with the director of another organization interested in UFOs, the Midwest (later Mutual) UFO Network (MUFON). Director Walt Andrus opened a file on the Aurora story and Case began giving him regular updates by mail and phone. In a letter on *Times-Herald* stationery written to Andrus on May 31, Case told Andrus he had sent "a complete file" on the Aurora case to renowned UFO researcher Dr. J. Allen Hynek, who had transformed from early skeptic to founder of the Center for UFO Studies. The reporter wrote:

"After the scientific findings of the analysts are in we would consider it an 'honor' and one hell of a boost if both you as MUFON national director and Dr. Hynek could comment on the effort and whether you consider the evidence substantial enough to go ahead with a firm effort to secure an exhumation order…"

MUFON had agreed to take the lead in seeking that order. The Oklahoma City UFO group headed by Hewes had been edged out of the story. Andrus' replies to Case are not posted on MUFON's Web site, but by midsummer, Andrus had scheduled a visit to Dallas. To spare him the price of a motel room, Case had found a couple who would put him up for free.

On July 8, the reporter typed a four-page, single-spaced memo for Andrus. The document, written on a Sunday and presumably Case's day off assessed the pros and cons of the Aurora case. Even if written on his own time, the memo constituted a serious breach of journalistic ethics in that Case was coaching Andrus on how to respond to questions posed by other reporters.

Aside from being a talking paper for Andrus, Case's memo—among the Aurora-related papers posted for all to see on MUFON's Web site—is the best summary of his take on the case. The reporter listed six points in his brief for the UFO crash having actually occurred, but they can be boiled down into four:

1. Physical evidence. The metal recovered by Kelley had tested out as pure tin, a scientist for the American Smelting Company saying he could give no reason why pure tin should have been at that spot in Wise County, Texas. Analysis of other metal samples found on the old Proctor place was still pending.
2. Statements from Aurora old-timers. These included a statement from Aurora resident C. C. Stephens that his father, James Stephens, had witnessed the crash and 91-year-old Mary Evans' recollection that her family and friends had talked about the crash.
3. The mysterious grave marker. Locals said the stone with the unusual markings had rested over the mystery grave for sixty-five to seventy years and "obviously this was no 'fake.' " The stone had been stolen as a result of all the publicity the case had been receiving, but it had been photographed before it went missing.
4. The multiple sightings of 1897. "[The Aurora case] cannot be divorced from the fact it was one of more than 500 airship sighting reports published in Dallas and Fort Worth newspapers from April 14 thru April 27, 1897."

The memo also shows that Case knew the party was over. The Aurora Cemetery Association had turned down MUFON's offer to conduct the exhumation with no media or bystanders present. The people of Aurora were not going to budge on the exhumation matter.

"We can go no further in Aurora," Case wrote.

In a way, the reporter-cum-ufologist saw that as a good thing. "Perhaps this works to MUFON's advantage. It leaves us 'deducting' from incomplete information blocked by the association's closing the cemetery..."

Case had become a believer that a UFO really had crashed at Aurora, possibly envisioning himself as the man who would finally prove that the world had been visited by aliens.

"There is no question a crash occurred," he continued in the memo. "There is no question a mystery grave has been in Aurora Cemetery since the incident. And evidence links them together...you can't explain away the evidence and the grave as 'just a hoax.' Hayden [sic] obviously worked from fact...We believe Hayden [sic], like Henry Ford, Thomas Edison and other pioneers in their fields, was ridiculed and maligned simply because the residents were admittedly frightened and wanted nothing to do with the unnatural event."

Despite Case's machinations, nothing further came of the Aurora investigation. While Case apparently believed the story, most people did not. Indeed, a close reading of Haydon's dispatch shows elements of tongue-in-cheek humor, such as noting the crash destroyed Judge Proctor's flower garden and elevating the local blacksmith to a position in the U.S. Signal Service. (Only Dallas and Fort Worth were large enough communities at the time to even have a Signal Service office, the forerunner of the modern National Weather Service.)

In referring to the other sightings, Haydon as much as admits that he gained inspiration from them and possibly from one other incident overlooked by all previous tellers of the Aurora tale: Turns out that the Aurora spaceman had not been the first mysterious visitor given a pauper's burial in the small Wise County town. A long-forgotten newspaper story suggests a factual origin for Haydon's spaceman being given a "Christian burial" by Wise County.

On May 6, 1896, Aurora resident Brown White set out to look for a couple of mules in a pasture west of town. Before he could find his animals, he walked up on what the story called "the putrid remains of a human being."

White immediately got in touch with Justice of the Peace J.S. Proctor. The judge, along with "a number of citizens," hurried to the scene to hold an inquest. Proctor and several of the other residents recognized the clothing on the body as the attire seen on a "total stranger" who had appeared in Aurora on April 23. After burning "every scrap of paper about his valise or person," the man had gone to a dense thicket off the road and shot himself in the head with a .38 caliber revolver. The man's unidentified remains were buried in the Aurora Cemetery the next day.

Less than a year later, Haydon filed his story about the airship crash and the unidentified pilot's funeral at the expense of the county.

Researchers have not turned up much information on the three key figures in the Aurora story—correspondent Haydon, Proctor and Weems.

A cotton buyer, Haydon is said to have been a frequent contributor to newspapers. But a search of the Dallas *Morning News* digital archives reveals neither other dispatches under his name nor any biographical information. More likely, Haydon wrote for the Aurora *News*, no copies of which are known to be extant, and the Wise County *Messenger*. Wise County historian Etta Pegues, who wrote a book on the Aurora community, read enough of Haydon's writing, including poems he wrote, to conclude:

"Imagination was his best asset, and this he used to carry to fruition his day dreams. One particular characteristic was that of supersedure. He wanted to excel, to stand out in importance above others. Perhaps this made him a bit of an egotist."

While he may have had a swelled head, Haydon also knew more than his share of disappointment and personal tragedy. Depleted soil and the boil weevil ate away at his success in the cotton business. An epidemic of "spotted fever" claimed his wife and two children. They are supposedly buried in the Aurora Cemetery, but a 2001 inventory of 1,540 grave markers in the cemetery does not show anyone with the surname of "Haydon." Neither does a Web site listing 27 million gravesites reveal Haydon's final resting place. Reportedly, Haydon moved to California, keeping up with his old friends by subscribing to the Wise County *Index*, a newspaper published at Boyd, the next closest small town to Aurora.

As for Proctor, though he had deep roots in the area (a J.A. Proctor settled in Wise County in 1854), whatever happened to him also remains a mystery. First elected justice of the peace for the county's fifth precinct in 1892, the judge held office for a decade. After that, he drops from the record. While Wise County cemetery records list several burials of likely relatives, the final resting place of Judge Proctor is not known.

A logical assumption is that as Aurora dried up and almost literally blew away, Proctor left town for more prosperous venues just as Haydon had done.

Finally, Weems was not a military officer, but Aurora's village smithy. His marble grave marker notes he was born in July 1842 and died in June 1925, the days of either month not given.

Bill Case, the man who tried to prove the Aurora UFO was real, died in 1974. Tolbert made it to 1984, not quite long enough to see his old newspaper's long-time rival, the *Times-Herald*, publish its final edition on December 9, 1991.

The legend of the spaceman lives on in DVDs of a 1986 movie called "Aurora Encounter," starring Jack Elam. A hybrid "B" Western and "B" science fiction movie, "Aurora

Encounter" was filmed in Ferris, sixty-eight miles from Aurora. Written by Jim McCullough, Jr., and directed by his father, the ninety-minute film further fictionalizes a fictional story. Borrowing on the success of "ET: The Extra-Terrestrial," the movie's script has the spaceman survive the crash—for a time. The good people of Aurora befriend the little guy, but trouble rides to town when the governor sends in a no-nonsense, trigger-happy Texas Ranger to find out what's going on.

With the passage of time, the Aurora legend has continued to grow. James L. Choron claimed in a 2004 article for the Web site texasescapes.com that the hapless alien injured in the crash may have lived for a time, cared for by a local doctor who did all he could to save him. He wrote: "Persistent rumors have circulated about a diary kept by the doctor, which disappeared in the late 1940s or early 1950s, when a team of United States Air Force officials made an examination of the crash site and collected all remaining evidence, both on the site and from private individuals."

Three years later, Fort Worth *Star-Telegram* reporter Eyder Peralta wrote: "Someone…says the alien didn't die in the crash. It survived and drank whiskey and played poker with the locals—until the Texas Rangers got wind of it and shot it dead." The journalist did not name that someone.

She did quote Rosalie Gregg, executive director of the Wise County Historical Society, the go-to person for questions about the spaceman story. "It didn't happen," are the three words Gregg uses at the beginning of her standard response to inquiries.

Gregg believes Haydon wrote the original newspaper story to bring attention to a town already in its economic death throes after having been bypassed by the railroad. To bolster her case, she has a taped interview with a man who was eleven in the spring of 1897, old enough to remember if a spaceship had crashed in the small town. But he said nothing happened.

"Also," Gregg told the reporter, "if it had happened, it would have been all over the Decatur newspapers." But those newspapers do not contain a word about a reported "airship" crash and the death of its occupant.

At first, Gregg continued, she saw the story as harmless folklore. But it attracted too many people as weird in their own way as any creature from outer space. They tromped all over the graves—marked and unmarked—in the town cemetery and even stole the alien's purported (by some) headstone. Even taped interviews of Aurora old-timers have turned up missing from the Wise County museum in nearby Decatur.

"Once people started getting hurt," Gregg said, "I didn't think [it was fun] anymore."

But the growth of the Internet has assured the Aurora spaceman's place in the cosmos—at least cyberspace. Typing the two words "Aurora spaceman" into the Google search engine nets nearly 400,000 results. So, just like Haley's Comet, the story of the Aurora spaceman endures, spinning in a seemingly perpetual orbit only to periodically reappear in the old or new media to amuse or baffle another generation.

CHAPTER 4:
BRIGHT LIGHTS, BIG MYSTERIES

Teenagers may not dance in Anson, but lights sure do.

Anson, population 2,556, sits at the intersection of Highways 180 and 83/277, about twenty miles northeast of Abilene. A mid-19th-century frontier outpost called Fort Phantom Hill predated it as the seat of Jones County.

Calling Anson a conservative West Texas town would be like calling Michael Dell well off. The town remains best known for municipal ordinances that regulate dancing so tightly that classes graduating from Anson High School rent out-of-town halls for their proms. Nearby Abilene, though fifty times larger, shares Anson's pious bent. Nary a liquor store can be found within the city limits of either community. Abilene's three institutes of higher learning—Abilene Christian (ACU), Hardin Simmons, and McMurry universities—are all church affiliated. Fearing that professors or deans might recognize their cars parked outside the city's "private clubs," students have been known to drive ninety miles southwest to San Angelo for Saturday nights on the town.

In short, young folks in this part of the state do not have much to do. At least they have those lights.

"I have personally seen the lights on three or four occasions," said Anson native Kevin Ansley. "That is just one of the things you do if you grow up there."

A typical viewing party consists of a few carloads of teenagers or young adults. (Average car occupancy may vary depending on whether it is date night.) Such groups venture east of town and travel down a country road to Mt. Hope Cemetery, a couple of miles north of Highway 180.

"Every time I viewed the lights, we chanted 'Little light, little light, come to me' over and over again. At some point, the light would appear and begin to move closer and closer to you, which always made the people there for the first time really nervous—you were never sure if it was a car, plane, UFO, or what," Ansley recalled. "The light, of course, never actually got to us—it would simply disappear as suddenly as it appeared."

Now a successful Amarillo businessman with teenagers of his own, Ansley believes some things in the universe cannot be explained. But he is fairly certain the lights he saw in his hometown were nothing more than headlamp reflections from cars on Highway 277. He adds a couple of important details about the typical sighting: "First, I never went there sober. A lot of people did, but most were not. Second, viewing the Anson Lights is almost a rite of passage for ACU students. If you meet someone who attended ACU and didn't take a trip to see the lights, they are almost certainly total nerds or shut-ins."

Anson is just one lesser-known vortex of an unexplained global phenomenon. Professor Yoshi-Hiko Ohtsuki of Tokyo's Waseda University devoted his professional career to studying so-called ball lightning, and his research reveals more sightings of "fireballs" in Texas than anywhere. Spooky lights in places like Six Mile Creek near Enchanted Rock and Bailey's Prairie near Angleton have inspired Texas ghost stories for generations.

Texas' two most famous mystery light locations—Marfa and Saratoga—share little in common besides sparse populations and orientation near thirty degrees latitude.

The Marfa Lights

Accounts of strange lights flitting around the Big Bend stretch back as far as human memory and folktales can take us.

Across the Rio Grande in Ojinaga, Native Americans scared their children into good behavior by telling them the lights glinted off a web spun by a giant spider between Chinati Peak and the Cerrito de la Santa Cruz range. The arachnid dropped down and punished naughty youth as they slept, according to the legend. Recognizing a good morality tale when they heard one, Franciscan friars later adapted the story for their own purposes.

The Marfa Lights have puzzled the denizens of far West Texas since pre-Columbian times. (Photo courtesy of *TEXAS HIGHWAYS*.)

Spanish exploration and colonization brought legends linking the mystery lights to buried treasure. Spaniards enslaved Indians, forced them to mine gold near San Carlos, Mexico, then buried them with it in the Marfa area. Their ghosts now dance above the treasure, or so the story goes.

45

Railroads began stretching across the American West in the last quarter of the 19th century. Steam engines required water stops at regular intervals, and Marfa began as a place to quench an iron horse's thirst. The few Anglos hardy enough to step off the train and put down roots in the area had plenty of time to watch the sky and inevitably saw some unusual things.

The historical marker at the official Marfa Lights View Park credits Robert Ellison with the first "recorded" sighting in 1883, only two years after the town's establishment. The settler spotted the lights while driving cattle across Paisano Pass and at first mistook them for Apache campfires. In fact, conflicts between the Apaches and immigrants of European descent gave rise to one of the most enduring Marfa Lights legends.

O.W. Williams, a surveyor who widely traveled the Big Bend region in the 1880s, first heard it as a campfire story told by a Mexican crewmember, Natividad Lujan. Williams jotted down the story in a journal, and his grandson Clayton read it during a dedication ceremony for the aforementioned historical marker a century later. (Oilman/rancher/businessman Clayton Williams narrowly lost the 1992 gubernatorial race to Ann Richards after making an unfortunate joke comparing the weather to a certain violent and unmentionable act.) Williams and his family still own large tracts in the Big Bend area and donated some land when the Texas Department of Transportation expanded the Marfa Lights View Park in 2003. The new shelter—improved with paved parking and restrooms—sits on U.S. Highway 90 about nine miles east of town.

The journal entry written by Clayton Williams' grandfather tells the story of Alsate, the last Mescalero Apache leader in the region. After a lifetime of raids and run-ins with Mexican authorities, the Rurales captured Alsate, executed him, and scattered his followers into to slavery. In one variation of the story, Alsate escapes and lives out his life in the Chisos, or "ghost," Mountains. Some believe the lights commonly seen there are Alsate's ghost.

Each subsequent generation projected its own imaginative anxiety onto the Marfa Lights:

- In Pancho Villa's day, the lights were thought to be lanterns guiding his nocturnal mule trains.
- World War I turned them into the headlights of trucks delivering supplies across the border as Germans amassed to invade the United States.
- During the next World War, they became German reconnaissance planes, Hitler's ghost searching for prisoners of war held at Fort D. A. Russell, or the results of laser-fusion weapons tests gone horribly awry.

During World War II, the Army Air Corp established Marfa Army Air Field as a training base in Mitchell Flat, the area just south of the Marfa Lights View Park. Some of the officers seemingly spent as much time chasing mystery lights as preparing young flyers to fight. Soldiers fired on the lights, bombed them, and even dropped flour on them in vain attempts to make their sources visible. Eventually, the Army divided the valley into sectors. Using range finders and radios, men on the ground and in the air tried to pinpoint the lights, which always disappeared or moved before planes or jeeps could catch up to them.

From time to time, professors from Sul Ross State University in Alpine and groups from outside the region attempted to find scientific explanations. Surveyors sent by the Army in 1918 and 1919 had no better luck at pinpointing the lights than their successors did a quarter century later. Some who led short-term surveys left convinced the lights are nothing more than headlights from highways and ranch roads. When NASA and the Air Force came at the height of the 1950s

47

UFO scare, they trotted out their typical swamp-gas and mineral-deposit explanations.

Those who have conducted more in-depth studies, however, find that the longer one watches the lights, the more difficult they become to explain.

In 1973, a pair of geologists working in the area spent about three months studying the lights. They felt inclined to accept the headlight theory until they set out to get a closer look at three orbs behaving strangely in the Chinati Mountains. They drove off down a dirt road, cut their headlights, and were rewarded with a close encounter. Basketball-sized lights came within a few hundred feet of their car. One, they reported, seemed to hover intelligently in the middle of the road before moving off to the east.

Those lucky enough to see true mystery lights in the Big Bend usually spot them from afar, against mountainous backdrops. Several small ranges can be seen across Mitchell Flat. The lights often materialize out of thin air and disappear just as quickly. Some remain stationary. Others divide, dart about in a very uncarlike manner, and merge back together. White and yellow lights appear most commonly, but red and blue-green hues sometimes make a showing.

By chance or intent, a number of locals have gotten closer looks.

Marfa Junior High published a coloring book about the favorite local anomaly in the 1980s, and it sparked Judith M. Brueske's interest. Customers of the Alpine bookstore where she worked often retold second-hand accounts of spectacular sightings as they perused the pictures. Brueske wanted to hear these stories from the horses' mouths. She set out to collect reports from as many first-hand witnesses as she could, then she published them in her own booklet. A few people told her about light balls following them down Highway 90 or other local roads, or of watching the lights cross their paths.

One witness, Orallia Torres of Alpine, saw them on a trip home from El Paso in the mid-1970s. A van driver woke her and about a dozen other young passengers about 3 a.m. as they crossed the flat between Marfa and Paisano Pass. "Look at the lights!" the driver yelled.

Torres told Brueske she saw six basketball-sized orbs of various colors silently approach the van from the south.

"They came straight at us like a train, all bunched together," Torres said. The lights disappeared the instant they seemed to touch the van.

Texas Department of Transportation expanded the Marfa Lights View Park in 2003, giving tourists a safer and more comfortable vantage point for glimpsing Texas' most famous mystery lights. (Photo courtesy of *TEXAS HIGHWAYS*.)

James Bunnell, a retired aerospace engineer who worked on some of the Cold War's most high-profile defense and space projects, graduated from Marfa High School but never believed he had seen anything truly unexplainable until a November

2000 sighting from the view park. Since then, Bunnell has written two books about the lights and set up nine astronomy-quality video cameras at various locations in Mitchell Flat. They capture about 150,000 images each night.

"I would say that there are around two dozen light sources that look mysterious to the general public and most, but not all, of those can be explained," Bunnell said. "Some of those, for example mirages, are intriguing in their own right, but it is the ones that seem to defy all explanations that I find so interesting. Those small residual sets are truly mysterious and have characteristics that are indeed puzzling. They richly deserve further study because they do not fit our current understanding."

Bragg Lights

Visitors gazing across Mitchell Flat from Highway 90 see—as the old song goes—"miles and miles of Texas" and on into Mexico. Low-growing desert vegetation does not block anyone's view.

Texas' second-most-famous mystery lights location couldn't be more different. Indian tales long warned visitors to stay out of certain creepy pockets of East Texas' Big Thicket, but the ghost light reports did not begin surfacing until a railroad company cut a hole in the pines big enough to see through.

Santa Fe laid tracks between Saratoga and Bragg in 1901. A traveler could board the train in the morning and ride among logs, cattle, and oil cars to Beaumont, then back all in a day's time. By 1934, the line had outlived its usefulness, and Santa Fe pulled up the tracks.

According to Francis E. Abernethy's book *Tales from the Bick Thicket*, at least one old timer recalled seeing the lights as a child while the tracks were still in place. Abernethy retells the memories of a Big Thicket native whose father worked for the railroad. She, her mother, siblings, and a neighbor saw the lights one night after walking down to the tracks to meet her dad. They thought the world was ending.

Sightings became more common once the tracks were gone. Local hunters then used the right-of-way as a shortcut through some of the densest woods in the area. As with the cemetery road in Anson, Bragg Road became a favorite parking spot for the young and impassioned. And like the Marfa Lights, those that appeared in the Big Thicket shown in various colors, sometimes standing still, sometimes flitting about, shooting straight up, and even chasing cars.

As is the case with the other two mystery light hot spots described here, Deep East Texas is a place where youth seriously lacked diversions before the invention of videogames. During the dog days of August 1960, word of the Bragg Lights spread through the teenage grapevine to neighboring counties. Bored youth from miles around gathered in the evenings, sitting on car hoods and tailgates. Watching for something.

Kuntze *News* publisher-editor Archer Fullington could not ignore a natural and/or social phenomenon such as this. He and Mrs. Geraldine Collins of Saratoga undertook an investigation of the Bragg Lights. The pair published their findings until the lights' fame spread throughout East Texas and beyond. Greater crowds converged. People of all persuasions came to shoot at, chase, and test the lights in various ways. A minister who shared the views of the railman's daughter preached of end times from atop his car. Again, dismissive investigators wrote off the lights as reflections from car headlights on a nearby road.

Yet people keep seeing lights along Bragg Road, and some of them argue staunchly against the headlight theory. With tall pine trees thwarting long-range visibility, the Big Thicket mystery lights tend to be encountered at much closer range than their West Texas counterparts. More than one witness has reported the lights passing over car hoods and causing vehicles to stall. Here also, some feel the lights' interaction with humans hint at intelligence.

More rarely, East Texans report seeing strange lights elsewhere amid their swamps and forests. Sour Lake native Rob Riggs grew up listening to tales of Big Thicket weirdness and first spotted mystery lights himself as a teenager in 1964. He saw a large, glowing ball flying around Pine Island Bayou, not far from Bragg Road. The experience sparked a quest to learn more about the unexplained phenomena long rumored in Deep East Texas, including mystery lights and the Big-Footlike "Wild Man." In a 2001 book, Riggs reported his compass needle spinning as he and a friend staked out mystery lights where a cleared pipeline right of way intersects Bragg Road.

Some of the legends inspired by the Big Thicket lights echo those told across the state—tales of lost Spanish gold and murdered laborers, for example.

Other stories reflect history unique to East Texas. During the Civil War, Confederate soldiers set fire to the Big Thicket to flush out fugitives who did not want to fight for the South. The lights, some say, are bits of fire from the so-called Kaiser Burnout still flickering today.

However, most Bragg Road lore ties to the railroad that came and went. In one tale, the ghost of a railroad man searches the right of way for the head he lost in a train wreck. Another tells of a farmer so enchanted by the new railroad that he sold his property to work as a brakeman. He died soon after the railroad's abandonment, and his lonely spirit walks the roadbed swinging a lantern.

Bailey's Prairie

Another lesser-known mystery light hot spot traces its legend to Texas' earliest American settlers.

Stephen F. Austin may be the father of Texas, but when he arrived with his colonists in December 1821, he found cantankerous James Britton Bailey firmly entrenched east of the Brazos. The pioneer, who some accused of squatting, had arrived three years earlier. Acquiescing to the settler and his pistols, Austin made no serious effort to dislodge Bailey from the land.

Legend and historical fact mingle freely in tales of old Brit Bailey, but by all accounts, the man loved to fight and drink. He delighted in saloon brawls and challenged travelers to fisticuffs just for the sport of it.

Old-timers say Brit Bailey's spirit sometimes appears as a ghost light in the prairie that bears his name. (Photo courtesy of Renee Roderick.)

When Bailey died of a fever on December 6, 1832, he left a will containing specific and unusual instructions regarding his burial. Local historians agree the will instructed his friends to bury Bailey standing up and facing west, the direction he had continuously moved since leaving his North Carolina birthplace. Less definitive stories variously claim he also demanded to be buried with guns, bullets, a powder horn, a favorite hunting dog, and/or a jug of whiskey. Legend holds that last request in that list was not honored, either because Bailey's mistreated slaves stole and drank the distilled spirits, or because his wife forbade burying him with it.

No one traveling west of Angleton could miss Bailey's home. He built it on the highest ground in the area and painted it red. Ann Raney Thomas, whose husband John bought the house after Bailey died, wrote the first account of Brit's ghost causing mischief. She claimed Bailey's full-formed apparition appeared to the couple on two occasions when they separately tried to sleep in the room and bed where the pioneer died. Slaves on the plantation told the Thomases they always milked the cows before dark to keep Bailey's ghost from turning it sour.

Brit Bailey stands in his grave somewhere near this roadside historical marker in Brazoria County. (Photo courtesy of Renee Roderick.)

According to author and historian Catherine Munson Foster, a member of her own venerable family first reported the mystery lights in the 1850s. Colonel Mordello Munson lived at the edge of Bailey's Prairie. One evening in the fall, Munson's dogs alerted him and a friend to a fireball floating some four miles away. The two saddled their horses and chased the light around all night, but it disappeared every time they drew near.

A black man named General Branch, who claimed to have been a slave but lived well into the 20th Century, claimed the light appeared every seven years in the late fall, and the Munson family's experience supports that. Robert Munson reported seeing the light twice—as a young man in 1939 and again in the same place in 1946.

As the horse-and-buggy days gave way to the automobile era, the ghost lights occasionally frightened motorists by appearing in the middle of a highway next to the prairie. But Foster lamented in her 1977 book *Ghosts along the Brazos* that as the countryside developed, the Bailey's Prairie light seemed to appear less frequently and less brilliantly. But if he holds to General Branch's schedule, 2009 would be the year to keep a light on and a glass frosted for old Brit's ghost.

Scientific Explanations?

Riggs, Brueske, and Bunnell agree that Texas' mystery lights cannot be all attributed to a single source or cause. The vast majority of those spotted by the untrained eye may actually originate from headlights. When subjected to scientific scrutiny, the sources of most can be identified. But as is the case with UFOs in general, a small but intriguing percentage cannot.

Bunnell began setting up video cameras on Mitchell Flat in 2003. He now checks images from three sites aimed at some of the mystery lights' favorite haunts. Single, wide-field cameras shoot video from two locations, while seven with variable-magnification lenses work together at Bunnell's Owlbert outpost, so named because several of the night birds call it home.

"Cameras in use today have incredible sensitivity. Thanks to image stacking and variable light gain, they can almost see in the dark," Bunnell explained. "They are capable of seeing satellites in orbit and are able to capture glow from the center of our galaxy."

Bunnell has caught some pretty amazing things on videotape, including meteors and rare upper-atmosphere lightning. One of his cameras shot the only image of giant jet lightning ever taken over North America.

Yet these highly unusual astronomic and atmospheric events do not account for everything Bunnell's cameras have picked up. The list of proposed explanations for truly mysterious lights grows long.

Swamp gas

The notion of flammable gasses seeping out of the ground sounds quite plausible for the Big Thicket, but Marfa has been swamp free for millions of years. Yet the late Big Bend matriarch Hallie Stillwell always associated them with rainy or damp periods. She reported seeing ghost lights throughout the region, not just on Mitchell Flat. Others have spotted them in typically dry weather, and Bunnell has not been able to determine any pattern of when the lights might appear. But "cienegas," the name given to a mountain range south of Alpine, means "marshes" in Spanish.

Mirages

Several publications over the past half-century have printed these poetic directions to the Big Bend, attributed to an anonymous cowboy:

You go south from Fort Davis until you come to the place where rainbows wait for rain, and the big river is kept in a stone box, and water runs uphill. And the mountains float in the air, except at night, when they go away to play with other mountains.

The old cowboy's description may be more literary than literal, but researchers believe the last sentence offers a likely explanation for some mystery lights. Remember the "temperature inversion" explanation so routinely offered by the Air Force to explain UFOs during the Cold War? Turns out it is a bona fide natural phenomenon that gives viewers glimpses of things just over the horizon, and sometimes even farther away. Air is usually warmest at the earth's surface and cooler at higher elevations. Sometimes cool and warm air trade places. In doing so they can bend, distort, and reflect light in ways that cause people dozens or hundreds of miles away to see things they should not be able to see. Temperature inversions can also create multiple images of the same object and break light up into different wavelengths of color, scientists say.

Temperatures drop quickly when night falls in the desert, and the peaks and valleys of the Big Bend create pockets where cool air can become trapped at lower elevations. Mirages are common. Bunnell found one account written by Gene Douglas in the July 28, 1976, edition of the Pecos *Enterprise*:

> I'm wondering if there could be any connection between those lights and an effect I've seen between here and Fort Stockton...Shortly after sunrise, coming from Stockton to Pecos, you can sometimes see Pecos about 20 or 30 miles before the town actually comes within sight...As you come close, you'll dip behind a hill and topping it,

the city is gone. A few miles later, it emerges again, looking completely different. As you come nearer, buildings will stretch or disappear one by one, and eventually the whole town disappears again.

If mirages caused by temperature inversions do make faraway lights dance around the Big Bend at night, they offer an explanation no less amazing than the mystery they solve.

Slow electric discharges

St. Elmo's fire could be called a traveler's companion. Sailors witnessed the unnerving lights shooting out from mast tips and named it for their patron saint. Pilots also watch St. Elmo's fire lick the tips of their wings.

It's an awe-inspiring sight, but St. Elmo's fire is really just static electricity. The friction of pulling a sweater over your head on a cold, dry day generates enough static electricity to make your hair stand up. In Marfa, where the air is almost always dry and temperatures can drop precipitously at night, cowboys have seen it emanating from cattle horns and fence posts.

On a much larger scale, friction and pressure on rocks in fault zones can cause mountaintops to emit lights in the form of auras, beams, or balls. This phenomenon is called piezoelectricity. British author Paul Devereux fleshed out this theory in his book *Earth Lights Revelation*, in which he plotted a higher-than-average number of UFO sightings near geologic faults.

Unusual lights have often been sighted before, during, and after earthquakes. However, Devereux posits that such drastic fault movement is not necessary to generate piezoelectric lights. The sighting that began the mid-1900s UFO craze, he notes, occurred in the Cascade Mountains, part of the Pacific's geologically hyperactive "ring of fire."

West Texas may not be all that geologically active, but the Lone Star State's biggest recorded earthquake occurred there in 1931. A temblor measuring 6.0 on the Richter scale rattled the Big Bend, with an epicenter in Valentine. A smaller quake centered only thirty-one miles from Mitchell Flat shook the area in 1995, Bunnell writes.

East Texan Riggs agrees that some mystery lights seen near Marfa may be piezoelectric in nature. He witnessed mountain peak discharge himself across the border in the Chihuahuan Desert. By contrast, he likens the Big Thicket to a "huge, half-baked mud pie" not subject to much subsurface friction.

Ball Lightning

This light phenomenon became another catchall that government officials used in the Cold War to dismiss things they either did not understand or did not want to explain. The problem is that nobody can say exactly what ball lightning is, even though science begrudgingly acknowledges its existence. And professor Ohtsuki believes the Air Force may have been right in some cases. He told the Houston *Chronicle* he thinks up to 80 percent of all UFOs may be ball lightning.

Like some of the upper-atmosphere flashes Bunnell catches with his Mitchell Flat cameras, ball lightning is so exceedingly rare that it has not been studied much by scientists. Those who have seen it usually describe it as round, but it can vary greatly in size and color. A few reports have documented ball lightning appearing inside buildings and airplanes.

Unlike St. Elmo's fire and mountain discharges, ball lightning moves around unpredictably instead of emanating from a fixed object (or slow-moving cow). Few believe, however, that it can explain the Marfa Lights. For one thing, the phenomenon is usually associated with storms, and the

Marfa Lights can be seen on clear nights. Ball lightning witnesses commonly smell foul odors and hear hissing sounds—sometimes loud, terminal bangs. Such unpleasantness is not reported in Mitchell Flat.

Phosphorescent minerals

At least one airplane pilot noticed a patch of faintly glowing rock or dirt a few miles south of Highway 90, but it can only be seen "if it's as dark as the inside of your hat at midnight," according to Brueske's booklet.

Those who have studied Texas ghost lights doubt bright minerals are to blame, seeing as how rocks do not move around much.

Glowing Wildlife

Storytellers in a West that can still be wild at times seldom let mere facts stand in the way of a good tale. Where would the mythological jackalope be without campfire orators (and a few good taxidermists)? Could its cousin, the glow-worm infested jackrabbit, be lighting things up? Some have hopped to that conclusion.

It's not surprising that a few locals might find zoological explanations somewhat plausible. According to Brueske, long-time Big Bend photographer and lay historian William D. Smithers speculated in the Alpine *Avalanche* a few decades past that mystery lights seen after a good rain might be the result of moisture combining with phosphates in bat guano.

Magnetospheric Particles

At the time Bunnell wrote his second Marfa Lights book, *Night Orbs*, his leading theory involved charged particles filtering into the earth's atmosphere from its outer magnetosphere, or the magnetic field that protects our planet from all kinds of damage.

Solar winds flowing past the magnetosphere give us the Northern Lights, and particles spewed from the sun can disrupt electrical grids and equipment on earth. Bunnell thought particles of plasma from space caught within the earth's magnetic field might light up if they made it near as Marfa. But once he placed more cameras in the field, he discounted the theory.

"My view has changed for a couple of reasons," he explained. "First, I am now inclined to believe that overcrowding of the inner radiation belt is relieved by electrical storms pulling trapped particles into the atmosphere (I suspect that is the explanation for sprites); and second, spectral studies of mystery lights have shown them to have continuous spectra, and that means that they are not plasma lights."

Better Stories

If science cannot definitively explain Texas mystery lights, that just leaves more room for imagination.

- Most of the slumber-party ghost stories told about the Anson Lights share a common theme. In them, a pioneer woman waits for one or more sons to return from a wood-chopping errand, or to walk home in perilous conditions. She expects lantern light to signal the return of her offspring. But the light never appears, and now her ghost wanders the old cemetery road, searching. Headlights flashed three times in the right direction summon her spirit—and the ghost lights.

- An enduring Mexican belief that possibly predates Spanish colonization is that people watching the Marfa Lights actually see novice *brujas*, or witches, crashing against the mountains while learning to fly.

- Jack Reed believed the Marfa Lights might be Satan. He hails from Shafter in Chinati Mountains, the heart of

Marfa Lights territory. He has seen them roll up mountainsides and linger near homes. "The Bible says that Satan made himself a light and that his ministers are also light," Reed told Brueske. "And in the Bible they're supposed to form a false Christ and bring him back in the sky, and I think this is what they're working on, these kinds of things." If a Canadian mining company has its way, many more people may soon see the light in Shafter. Rising silver prices prompted it to pay $43 million for the closed mines on which this near-ghost town was founded in the 1880s. The company, Aurcana, plans to put ninety people to work in Shafter by 2010.

- Richard McLaren, an Ohio transplant to Fort Davis, convinced a surprising number of people in the mid-1990s that Texas was still a sovereign nation, claiming it had been illegally annexed into the Union. He managed to get himself elected president of the Republic of Texas, but his delusional political career ended in standoff with state authorities in 1997. The clerks at Jeff Davis County Courthouse knew McLaren well. Among the mountains of frivolous paper he deposited in their care was a resolution creating the Foundation for the Advancement of Space Laws and Sciences. He believed the McDonald Observatory in Fort Davis channeled an underground energy source. McLaren's convoluted theory linked the Marfa Lights, UFOs, and Ronald Regan's Star Wars missile defense programs. The lights served as a beacon for extraterrestrial navigators.

Most folks who live nearest mystery lights content themselves with the unknown. Some fear scientific explanations would ruin their towns' lucrative notoriety. For example, such knowledge might put a damper on the Marfa Lights Festival hosted by the local chamber of commerce each Labor Day weekend.

"The Marfa Lights are a mystery," the late Stillwell once told a reporter. "Let 'em stay a mystery."

Bunnell disagrees.

"The people of Marfa can take comfort in knowing that the phenomena they call 'Marfa Lights' are genuine scientific puzzles," he said. "Skeptics will continue to loudly dismiss them as ordinary events, but the day will come when they are recognized and studied by our scientific community. When that starts to happen, Marfa and 'Marfa Lights' will achieve worldwide recognition and attention."

Until then, Texans will continue parking beside Highway 90, Bragg Road, and the old Anson graveyard with friends, family, complete strangers, and coolers full of their favorite beverages. They will speak excitedly in hushed tones as they watch amazing orbs of light dance in the night.

Do we really need to solve the Marfa Lights mystery? In the words of Clayton Williams (taken completely out of context from the joke that helped end his short political career), maybe we should all just "relax and enjoy it."

And who knows? If we turned off our TVs, snuffed out the city lights, and looked up long enough, maybe we could see mystery lights in our own backyards.

CHAPTER 5:
THE ROSWELL INCIDENT:
A UFO LEGEND FROM OUTER TEXAS

Brigadier General Roger M. Ramey faced reporters on July 8, 1947, in arguably the most unusual press conference of his—or possibly any—military career. The commander of the Eighth Air Force burst a bubble of excitement when he told those gathered at Fort Worth Army Airfield (FWAA) that a crashed weather balloon—not an alien spaceship—scattered debris found across a remote pasture several hundred miles away.

Ramey's surreal press conference did not mark the first time, nor the last, that a Texan would attempt to clean up a neighbor's mess. In this case, the Texan was a rodeo cowboy from Denton who became a decorated command pilot. His chance association with the aeronautically odd spurred the New York Times *to nickname Ramey the Air Force's "saucer man" as he continued shooting down extraterrestrial theories into the 1950s. The mess in question fell out of the sky about eighty-five miles northwest of Roswell, New Mexico, a cactus-filled region to which Texas relinquished claim after the independent nation was annexed into the United States. Ramey's damage control worked for about thirty years, until the paranoia that often grows in information vacuums gave birth to one of the world's best-known and most enduring conspiracy theories.*

Ultimately, neither the Air Force nor the CIA could deny that something happened in Roswell. Well over a half-century later, exactly what that something was is still up for debate in some quarters. And with that ambiguity comes tourism opportunity for the small city just down the road from Carlsbad Caverns.

General Roger Ramey (left) and Colonel Thomas Jefferson DuBose pose in Ramey's office with debris recovered from Roswell. (Photo courtesy of *Fort Worth Star-Telegram Photograph Collection*, Special Collections, The University of Texas at Arlington Library, Arlington, Texas.)

A fierce thunderstorm blew through southeastern New Mexico on the night of June 14, 1947. The next day, rancher

W.W. "Mac" Brazel rode out on horseback to check his sheep. Part of his flock grazed on the J.B. Foster ranch, where near the old ranch house, he noticed a trail of strange looking tinfoil, rubber, sticks, and paper.

Brazel had sheep on his mind that day, so he did not take much notice of what some would later come to consider intergalactic space junk. After mulling things over and telling his family about what he saw, Brazel returned to the site on July 4 with his wife and two children. They spent Independence Day gathering debris.

Brazel would later tell the Roswell *Record* that he first began to wonder if his find might be flying saucer wreckage when he heard a news report the next day about strange sightings across the country. The following Monday, he mentioned his theory to Chaves County Sheriff George Wilcox while on a trip to town to sell wool.

Wilcox in turn called Roswell Army Air Field (RAAF) and spoke to intelligence officer Major Jesse A. Marcel. Brazel then took Marcel and Counter-Intelligence Corp agent Sheridan Cavitt to the crash site. There, the group recovered the rest of the wreckage. They took it back to Brazel's home, where the men unsuccessfully tried to reconstruct it into a kite or anything else that seemed to make sense. The Air Force officials finally packed everything and up headed back to Roswell.

Strange Things Happen in New Mexico

In the years following World War II, the Cold War's chill settled across the country like a blanket of secrecy embroidered with the occasional thread of misinformation. After all, what the Soviets didn't know couldn't hurt us. And the more the U.S. military knew about our rival superpower, the better prepared we would be to respond to a nuclear threat.

New Mexico quickly became a Cold War hot spot. Some the nation's most secretive defense research took place at military installations in the sparsely populated and geographically forbidding desert state. Scientists at White Sands Missile Base developed the atomic bomb, and the 509th Bomb Group stationed at RAAF dropped two of them on Japan. The Balloon Branch at Alamogordo Army Air Field (AAAF) sent aloft high-tech devices designed to spy on the Russians. And late Air Force historian Bruce Ashcroft admitted that even he did not know what happened in Albuquerque. The bases worked on projects so hush-hush that officials sometimes did not share information with each other, let alone civilians. Inevitably, devices drifted over to neighboring facilities or onto private property. To this day, motorists traveling along U.S. Highway 380 sometimes encounter hours-long delays when the military blocks the road for missile tests at White Sands.

With similarly clandestine research taking place at other bases around the world, the UFO mania that took hold during the summer of 1947 does not seem surprising in hindsight. The Central Intelligence Agency (CIA) documented its first U.S. flying saucer report on June 24 of that year, when a private pilot spotted nine of them near Mt. Rainier in Washington State. A rash of sightings followed.

The week of July 4, 1947, broke a record for official UFO reports that held for five years, until a rash of sightings in Washington, D.C., overshadowed the Democratic National Convention of 1952. Reports of the Roswell occurrence shared headline space in the Albuquerque *Journal* with stories about sightings in Australia, South Africa, Denmark, England, Sweden, Oregon, Seattle, and San Francisco. Errant motorist Joseph H. Kurtiz of South Bend, Indiana, told arresting officers that he had to break the speed limit to keep up with the flying disc he was chasing, according to an International News Service brief. And Vice Admiral William H. Blandy, commander of Bikini Atoll nuclear tests, joked that at least the UFO sightings could not be blamed on his job. As they would for generations to come, scientists attributed the sightings to mass hysteria, retinal detachment, secret missile or aircraft test flights, natural phenomena, or atomic energy byproducts.

In later years, Major Jesse Marcel would publicly express his belief that this wreckage recovered from Roswell was "not of this world." He is pictured here during a press conference in General Roger Ramey's office at Fort Worth Army Air Field on July 8, 1947. (Photo courtesy of *Fort Worth Star-Telegram Photograph Collection*, Special Collections, The University of Texas at Arlington Library, Arlington, Texas.)

The Athletic Round Table of Spokane, Washington, the World Inventors Exposition of Los Angeles, and Chicago industrialist E.J. Culligan had put up a collective bounty of

$3,000 for spaceship evidence that summer. This fact prompted some skeptics to surmise that dollar signs may have motivated Brazel to contact the sheriff. Turning in a downed weather balloon, which New Mexicans often found, netted only a $5 reward.

A Puzzling Press Release

The story might have ended with Marcel and Cavitt's departure from Brazel's house if not for the first in a long series of what the Air Force would later recognize as public relations missteps. For reasons few know and even fewer understand, Roswell base commander Colonel William Blanchard called Lieutenant Walter Haut on the morning of July 8 and ordered him to issue a press release stating that the 509th had gained possession of a crashed disc.

Haut was no stranger to flying objects. He joined the Army Air Corp in December 1942, trained as a navigator, and went through bombardier school in Roswell before flying thirty-five missions in the Pacific theater. He finished the last years of his commitment to Uncle Sam as RAAF's public affairs officer (PAO).

In later years, Haut would suspect that Blanchard acted on orders from higher up when he instructed the PAO to write the press release. Like any good soldier, Haut did what his commanding officer instructed.

"I think people have a very difficult time understanding that when the colonel told a first lieutenant to do it, that first lieutenant didn't ask why or anything else, you just went ahead and did it," Haut recalled in a 1999 interview. "The 509th was a real unusual group. It was the only one in the world at that time capable of carrying and dropping the atomic weapons. There was a different attitude than just a run-of-the-mill bomb group…. Secrecy was part of the culture."

Regardless of his reasons for writing it, Haut hand delivered the press release to Roswell's two newspapers and two radio stations late that morning. Then he went home to lunch.

When Haut returned to the office, phones were ringing with calls from every corner of the globe. The calls followed him home when he left that evening. Reporters asked Haut to describe the disc, but he only knew what Blanchard had told him to write. "If he wanted me to have more information, he would have given it to me," Haut said.

Air Force officials quickly shipped the rubble off to Fort Worth. Within hours of Haut's release, Ramey stood before the press identifying it as the remnants of a weather balloon used in high-altitude tests. Marcel accompanied the debris to FWAA, where he and Ramey posed for photos with bits of it scattered across Ramey's office floor.

With all of its more senior shutterbugs busy with other assignments that day, the Fort Worth *Star-Telegram* pressed twenty-one-year-old photographer J. Bond Johnson into duty. The few photos he snapped in Ramey's office ran across the Associated Press wire the next day and would then gather dust for more than three decades before ufologists resurrected the "Roswell Incident." The much-studied photos would bring Johnson, by then a Methodist preacher, more than fifteen minutes of minor fame.

Other officers present at FWAA that day could not help but notice Marcel's enchantment with the flying-saucer notion. Based on this, UFO skeptic Peter Brookesmith questioned Haut's assumption that inspiration for the press release came from higher up the chain of command and suspected Marcel's influence instead. In his 1996 book *UFO: The Government Files*, Brookesmith reported that agent Cavitt, who visited the ranch with Marcel, thought the incident of so little consequence that he did not even file a report. Brookesmith also pointed out that the major in later years inflated tales of his World War II service far beyond reality.

The RAAF press release did not name Brazel, but by the afternoon of Ramey's press conference, an Associated Press photographer took the rancher's photo at the local radio station. Brazel soon regretted becoming a central figure in the ensuing international media frenzy. "I am sure that what I found was not any weather observation balloon," he told the local paper. "But if I find anything else besides a bomb they are going to have a hard time getting me to say anything about it."

Despite Brazel's doubts—and those of countless others in years to come— scientific and military experts still stick by Ramey's story. For example, the *Skeptical Inquirer* printed a story in 1995 featuring as its key witness Charles B. Moore, one of three then-surviving scientists who worked on top-secret Project Mogul. That operation was so clandestine that those working on parts of it were not even aware of complementary research being conducted by others.

> The Mogul project was so classified and compartmentalized that even Moore did not know the project's name [at the time].... The unclassified purpose of the project was to develop constant-level balloons for meteorological purposes. Its classified purpose was to try to develop a way to monitor possible Soviet nuclear detonations with the use of low-frequency acoustic microphones placed at high altitudes.

Moore and a team from New York University conducted balloon studies at nearby AAAF. He recognized some of the odd markings on Brazel's pasture trash as stylized designs that decorated reinforcing tape used in test balloons. Air Force personnel spotted common radar target markings on the wreckage as well.

Official Secrecy

The Texas general's explanation satisfied the general public, and the Roswell tale seemed to die a quick, if disappointing, death. But seeds of the story survived, and in the ensuing decades, these would grow into a full-fledged conspiratorial legend nourished in part by the CIA's false denials of any interest in Roswell or UFOs in general.

The flying-saucer frenzy of 1947 puzzled some government and military officials as much as it did civilians. In January of the following year, the Air Force established Project SIGN. This effort, run by the Technical Intelligence Division of the Air Material Command at Wright Field in Ohio, kept track of UFO sightings. Authorities initially feared that people might be seeing secret Soviet aircraft flying over the United States, but further study proved that nearly all UFO sightings could be attributed to hallucinations, mass hysteria, or misidentification of known aircraft or atmospheric phenomena. Of 12,618 sightings investigated and catalogued by the Air Force's Project Blue Book beginning in 1947, only 701 remained unidentified when the project closed on December 17, 1969. None were considered threats to national security.

But the Air Force found it difficult to combat the awe-inspiring notion that beings from other worlds might clandestinely visit Earth. Officials recommended scaling back UFO monitoring activities and mounted a PR campaign to convince the public that, given enough scrutiny, strange objects seen in the sky rarely remained unidentified for long. The Department of Defense also refused military assistance to any motion picture project that depicted extraterrestrial life.

Ever-vigilant CIA officials, however, felt a duty to investigate UFO reports on the extremely remote chance that interplanetary spacecraft might be lurking around our atmosphere. More plausibly, a CIA study group formed in 1952 postulated that the Russians might use UFO reports as a psychological warfare tactic or a means to overload the American air warning system while mounting a surprise nuclear attack. Characteristically, the CIA refused to admit its interest in UFOs. Personnel were forbidden from mentioning classified UFO studies. "This attitude would later cause the Agency major problems related to its credibility," National Reconnaissance Office historian Gerald K. Haines wrote in a 1997 paper published in *Studies in Intelligence*.

By the mid-1950s, some military and intelligence officers knew things they were not telling about unfamiliar objects crisscrossing American skies. Civilian reports of UFOs spiked as high-altitude U-2 reconnaissance aircraft took to the skies. While the Air Force truthfully attributed earlier sightings to terrestrial events, it began issuing intentionally misleading statements during this period. When air traffic controllers or commercial pilots spotted U-2s, the Air Force explained them away as temperature inversions, ice crystals, or other natural phenomena, according to Haines.

As public skepticism of official reports mounted, a patterned emerged: the Air Force would ask the CIA for permission to declassify legitimate studies and reports that presented logical explanations for UFO sightings, but the CIA refused to release anything with its name attached. Well into the 1970s, the CIA continued to falsely deny ever having studied UFOs. By the 1980s, CIA officials intentionally avoided creating documents related to UFOs that might later be subject to release under the U.S. Freedom of Information Act (FOI).

Suspicion of the official government line continued to foment in this information void. Some not inaccurately believed that the U.S. government—perhaps more than the Soviet Union—fueled the UFO phenomena.

Amid hundreds of mysterious sightings, most people seemed to accept the weather-balloon explanation for the junk Brazel found in his field. The story lay relatively dormant until the late 1970s, when Marcel told the *National Enquirer* he did not believe the wreckage he recovered was "of this world."

"Before that, the Air Force had never considered Roswell a UFO incident," historian Ashcroft said in a 1999 interview.

Enter the Undertaker

Marcel's revelation sparked new interest in Roswell and led to a spate of books by self-proclaimed ufologists. The galactically and conspiratorially open minded became even more intrigued in the late 1980s and early 1990s when W. Glenn Dennis began offering sketchy accounts of alien autopsies to television producers and UFO researchers.

Dennis claimed that back in 1947, he worked as a mortician at Roswell's Ballard Funeral Home. The mortuary provided both hearse and ambulance services for the community and occasionally the base. Dennis first publicly discussed his recollections of July 7, 1947, in the summer of 1989 with producers from *Unsolved Mysteries* and a Las Vegas television station. He claimed the mortuary affairs officer at RAAF called twice that day, first inquiring about the availability of child-sized coffins, then asking for advice on embalming bodies that had been exposed to the elements for a few days.

Later that day, Dennis reportedly responded to a call for an ambulance at a minor traffic accident involving a serviceman stationed at RAAF. At the base hospital, Dennis reported seeing unusual material inside some Army ambulances. The twenty-two-year-old mortician then looked around for an Army a nurse with whom he had cultivated an acquaintance, and he found her visibly shaken. Dennis claimed he later met the nurse at the officers' club, where she drew diagrams of odd little bodies on which Army doctors had performed preliminary autopsies. Officials then shipped the remains off to Ohio's Wright Field (which later became Wright-Patterson Air Force Base). The two would never meet again, according to Dennis' accounts. The nurse was abruptly reassigned, possibly to a station in London, he told interviewers.

Around the time Dennis began telling his story, others started coming forward with second- and third-hand tales of alien crashes and diminutive corpses. Aspiring authors solicited some of these accounts by publishing newspaper announcements, including one that ran in the Socorro *Defensor Chieftain* in November 1992. When Moore and an Air Force scientist responded with unsensational explanations for the events of July 1947, the authors who placed the ad dismissed the men as cogs in the government machine.

Throughout the 1980s and 1990s, those who retrieved decades-old memories about strange experiences in the New Mexico countryside talked of air craft crashes; figures that could have been bodies, dolls, or dummies; and mini-invasions by military personnel and equipment. Some authors believed the government knew about alien visits to Earth, while others debunked the notion.

The Air Force, meanwhile, fielded so many calls and FOI requests about Roswell that it conducted two exhaustive searches of its records.

The first research project culminated with 1994's *The Roswell Report: Fact vs. Fiction in the New Mexico Desert*, which focused on what did and did not happen in July 1947. Three years later, the Air Force published *The Roswell Report: Case Closed*, which postulated that the alien bodies some recalled seeing decades after the fact were really crash dummies dropped from high-altitude balloons. And, to skeptics at least, the latter report punched holes in Dennis' story large enough for a spaceship to fly through. Although the Air Force could not supply a definitive answer to the Roswell puzzle, its final report on the subject implied that hazy memories of weather balloons, crash test dummies, and aircraft accidents coalesced into what became the "Roswell incident."

Another "Crash"

One incident that helped keep the Roswell mystique alive evolved from mischievous hoax to felonious scam to gullible belief. With Brazel's balloon story fresh on New Mexican minds, a newspaper editor in the opposite side of the state decided to have a little fun in March 1948. Aztec sits near Pueblo ruins southeast of the Four Corners where New Mexico, Arizona, Colorado, and Utah converge. Perhaps the surrounding historical wonders of Anasazi kivas and cliff dwellings, combined with a lack of big-city entertainment opportunities, sparked George Bawra's imagination. Whatever his reasons or inspirations, Bawra published in the Aztec *Independent-Review* an eye-winking tale of flying saucers from Venus crash landing in the local desert. Dozens of papers around the country picked up the story in the following months.

A story like that—be it truth or fiction—proved too good to languish in rural New Mexico. A Hollywood actor and a pair of southwestern shysters made sure of that, according the skeptic Brookesmith.

Convicted conmen Silas M. Newton and Leo GeBauer incorporated the Aztec tale into a profitable scam, Brookesmith wrote. In 1947, Newton witnessed a UFO himself in Wyoming. He met GeBauer two years later, and the pair soon read news stories about a couple of prospectors who recounted seeing two small beings run from a crashed saucer in Death Valley, California. Newton had come up with a gadget he called the "Doodlebug" which he claimed could locate gold and oil deposits. The Death Valley story inspired him to attribute the technology to a downed alien craft. Newton and GeBauer would buy land cheap, demonstrate their apparatus, and sell it to less-than-shrewd marks. The story grew and changed as the two slipped from town to town, and Aztec eventually became the standard crash location.

Concurrently in California, actor Mike Conrad mulled an idea for a movie script about aliens establishing a base in Alaska. To create what would be called "buzz" these days, Conrad hired a promoter to impersonate an FBI agent. This undercover publicist planted rumors in the press that the government had videotape of a flying saucer crash that would be featured in Conrad's movie. Except for the crash location and the aliens' planet of origin, the bogus agent's tale mimicked Bawra's.

The Conrad and Newton versions converged on *Variety* columnist Frank Scully. Presenting himself as a Texas oilman and GeBauer as the mysterious scientist "Dr. Gee," Newton bent Scully's ear for months. When Scully read Conrad's planted stories, he apparently viewed them as corroboration of the conmen's tale.

Scully swallowed both yarns and featured the alleged Aztec crash in his 1950 book *Behind the Flying Saucers.* He described the downed craft in great detail, along with its perished crew of sixteen diminutive aliens in good dental health. Even though the crash victims were not native to this planet, Scully's "sources" somehow determined that they were all middle aged.

More fastidious researchers debunked Scully's story by the end of the decade, but a new generations of ufologist accepted the tale as fact by the 1980s.

The twisted path the Aztec tale took to acceptance in the minds of some modern-day believers proves what the Air Force concluded in its *Case Closed* report:

> The many Air Force
> activities cobbled together in the
> ever changing collage that has
> become the "Roswell Incident,"

> when examined in the clear light
> of historical research, revealed a
> remarkable chapter of the Air
> Force story. In the final analysis,
> this examination simply
> illustrates once again, that fact is
> indeed stranger, and often much
> more fascinating, than fiction.

The Air Force indeed considered the case closed after its 1997 report. Public affairs officers now refuse to speak on the record about Roswell and will not even anecdotally discuss whether information requests have waned in subsequent years.

But a good mystery cannot be killed just because official sources refuse to talk about it. Government silence, in fact, is part of what built the legend.

"From the public affairs side, it's an impossible situation," Ashcroft said. "Regardless of what you bring forward, people always say, 'But yeah, tell us what you haven't told us.' " Haines agreed in his CIA report: "No matter how much material the agency releases, and no matter how dull and prosaic the information, people continue to believe in an agency cover up and conspiracy."

Party Time

Haut and Dennis did their part to keep the Roswell story alive—and profitable. After his discharge from the Army, Haut tried his hand at selling insurance and real estate, ran a collections agency, and opened an art gallery. In 1991, he, Dennis, and local real-estate broker Max Littell founded the International UFO Museum and Research Center in Roswell.

By 1997, New Mexicans began to embrace the city's notoriety and the economic opportunities it promised. Jon "Andy" Kissner, then a New Mexico state representative, got into the act by proposing a witness protection program for anyone involved with spacecraft clean-up activities a half century earlier. And the city celebrated the 50th anniversary of Brazel's discovery in a big way with its first Roswell Encounter, which drew 40,000 visitors and filled motel rooms for 100 miles around.

The extraterrestrial business has proven so lucrative for Roswell, New Mexico, that the city erected alien-head street lamps, pictured here outside the International UFO Museum and Research Center. (Photo courtesy of the City of Roswell.)

Ultimately, the Roswell drama outlived its lead Earthling players. Haut's daughter, Julie Schuster, keeps the legend going as director of the museum her late father and his friends founded. Undoubtedly, a significant percentage of the 200,000 visitors the museum entertains each year make the short drive across the Texas state line from Odessa or El Paso.

The party continues each Fourth of July, still drawing 20,000 to 30,000 celebrants annually. True believers mix with revelers satisfied by an excuse to drink beer, dress up in tinfoil, or buy an Area 51 coffee mug.

Everyone gets into the act during the Amazing Roswell UFO Festival, held annually around July 4 to commemorate the 1947 "incident." (Photo courtesy of the City of Roswell.)

The 2007 event included an Alan Parsons Project concert and a speech by Stephen Bassett, founder of the X-PPAC political action committee. He felt a Democrat victory in the 2008 presidential elections would finally bring full government disclosure of long-withheld documents. Some ufologists hoped for a Hillary Clinton/Bill Richardson dream ticket.

The alien business has proven quite lucrative for Roswell, but it took awhile for some residents to come around to the "if you can't beat them, throw a party" viewpoint. "I have friends who are embarrassed by it, but I don't see that as much any more," said Elaine Mayfield, the city's zoo director and the 2008 UFO festival committee's vendor chairwoman. "Cities all over the world would die for the chance to have name recognition like we have."

In 2007, the city officially sponsored the festival for the first time. Roswell also adopted a new logo featuring a flying saucer and the words "Visitors Welcome." Alien-headed streetlights now keep watch over downtown, and the local McDonalds and Wal-Mart boast alien-themed décor.

Not to be left out, Aztec also sponsors a UFO gathering each March. The lineup for its 2008 symposium included Dr. Jesse Marcel Jr. and Timothy Good, a believer in Scully's work.

So all's well that ends well—even if it lands badly—in New Mexico. But even though the Air Force's weather-balloon-and-crash-dummies story seems plausible to most, many still wonder why Haut issued the press release that Ramey later disavowed in Fort Worth.

"I think there's not a good answer to that question," admitted Ashcroft. "No matter what the Air Force tries to do, people who believe in conspiracies will always go back to the initial report."

Chapter 6:
Attack on Camp Hood

In the late 1940s, the general public had no idea what was going on at a secret base across U.S. Highway 190 from Camp Hood, a sprawling Army installation in Central Texas established as a tank destroyer training camp during World War II.

Judging from newspapers of the day, the news media stood equally in the dark about activities in the vicinity of fast-growing Killeen, a once quiet cow town about an hour's drive north of Austin. Newspaper readers would have thought nothing but routine military training took place at the camp, the postwar home of the famed 2nd Armored Division, the late General George S. Patton's former outfit. Most articles were based on news releases issued by the base's public affairs office, routine items such as the one published in the Yuma *Daily Sun* in the summer of 1949 noting that a private from Yuma had recently been transferred to Camp Hood as a physical education instructor.

No one had any inkling that as the fourth decade of the 20th century neared its end some in the military had begun to wonder if the top-secret activities then under way at the post (not formally named Fort Hood until 1950) were being spied on by spacecraft. Either that or the Russians had developed some secret means of flying over the hush-hush installation.

That a civilian construction contractor was hiring men from coal mining states like Pennsylvania and Kentucky for a job near Camp Hood does not seem to have raised any eyebrows in Killeen, though no coal deposits existed on the federal reservation. In fact, only a few veins of that particular fossil fuel could be found anywhere in the Lone Star State.

Of course, the military saw to it that even those hired to work at the base were kept in the dark about the true nature of their job. All they knew was that they had signed on to blast a series of large tunnels into a hillside somewhere in the middle of Texas. The mostly imported labor pool had no idea that they were working on a top-secret endeavor that had nothing to do with mining. The military referred to it as Project 76.

Starting in the spring of 1947, this army of miners descended on a 7,000-acre tract (eventually expanded to 8,894 acres) six miles west of Killeen in Bell and Coryell counties. They noticed they had to pass by Camp Hood to get to the job site, but happy to be getting a good paycheck in a sluggish postwar economy, they must not have given it a whole lot of thought.

Years after the veil of governmental secrecy had finally been lifted, a retired contractor told a reporter with the Fort Hood *Sentinel* that the workers had drilled and blasted a network of tunnels through solid rock. In effect, they hollowed out what passed for a mountain in that part of Texas. Twenty feet wide and thirty feet high, the shafts went down eighty or more feet.

By the fall of 1947, workers with other skills began pouring tons of steel-re-enforced concrete inside the tunnels. An overhead rail system capable of transporting heavy loads was installed along with ventilation machinery, wiring, lighting, and security measures. Contractors also erected a series of concrete watchtowers and bunkers that ringed the high-fenced acreage.

A facility first known as Site Baker and later as Killeen Base became operational in 1948. Soon, in the dead of night, the Santa Fe Railroad began stopping long freight trains adjacent to the base and switching boxcars to a spur leading into the fenced compound. Noting that armed guards observed the off-loading operation, railroad personnel could only watch and wonder what sort of freight the cars carried.

Unknown to anyone but the highest levels of the U.S. military command and top officials with the relatively new Atomic Energy Commission, this remote area of Camp Hood had been transformed into one of only three nuclear weapons storage sites in the nation.

Postcard from Fort Hood, Texas

As of 1947, the U.S. arsenal consisted of only thirteen nuclear bombs, but the supply would be growing exponentially. The stockpile increased more than three-fold in 1948 to fifty-six devices and by the end of the decade, the U.S. military had 228 atomic weapons at its disposal. Initially the security-cloaked installation adjacent to Camp Hood held B4 bombs, the first mass-produced nuclear weapons. Later, Killeen Base included tactical nuclear weapons designed for battlefield use in the event Russia's Red Army rolled its tanks into Europe

84

and triggered World War III, a conflict even the most hawkish generals knew might precipitate the end of civilization.

Though Camp Hood proper was an open post, what happened at Killeen Base was strictly need-to-know and off-limits to the general public. Soldiers appeared to pop out of nowhere from underground to challenge anyone wandering too close to the site or even worse, somehow actually getting onto the reservation.

Once, Fort Hood lore has it, a couple of hapless deer hunters strayed onto the area, hunting rifles in hand. Soldiers in full combat gear quickly surrounded the startled pair and hauled them to a Jeep for a fast ride to headquarters. The Army held the men incommunicado for hours until intelligence agents had satisfied themselves that the two good old boys were not agents of Soviet dictator Joseph Stalin.

Incidents such as that stimulated fanciful rumors. People said the Army had built an underground airfield, where military planes could taxi straight into the side of a mountain to discharge or pick up some mysterious cargo. One wild tale had it that the United States had constructed a two-hundred-plus-mile subterranean channel from the base all the way to the Gulf of Mexico, a bombproof passage enabling the stealthy deployment of submarines armed with nuclear torpedoes.

Landlocked Killeen had not been transformed into a Navy base, but the part about airplanes handling secret cargo was at least partially correct. The military had constructed a 10,000-foot runway adjacent to Killeen Base, the genesis of what would become Robert F. Gray Air Force Base. The landing field could easily accommodate B-29 bombers, the delivery system for atomic weapons.

"One of my uncles worked out there and was not allowed to talk about anything he did," recalled Michael Adams, a University of Texas at Austin English professor whose father later served as Killeen's mayor. "My uncle's silence made him a character of mystery."

Those involved with the Armed Forces Special Weapons Project, which oversaw the weapons storage operation, generically rcfcrrcd to the Killeen facility and two similar sites either planned or under construction as Q Areas. The name came from the Atomic Energy Commission's highest security clearance level, Q. To get a Q clearance, federal employees or civilian contractors like Dr. Adams' uncle had to pass a thorough FBI investigation to make sure they had no connection to communism or any foreign government or posed any other sort of potential security risk.

With construction complete at Site Baker, the Army began stockpiling its growing nuclear arsenal at Camp Hood. While military brass in Killeen and at the Pentagon assessed the big picture of the world scene, rank and file GIs stationed at the secret Texas site had only the protection of the underground facility's perimeter to worry about. For them, that job amounted to routine peacetime soldiering, at least until March 6, 1949.

Something in the Sky

At 8:20 p.m. that late winter night, Sergeant Hubert Vickery and Private John Ransom saw something in the sky they had no means to challenge: An oblong, blue-white object moving southward in the airspace over the supposedly impenetrable facility. From the soldier's vantage point on the ground, whatever it was looked to be about two feet by one foot. Other patrol teams reported seeing something similar.

After midnight Private Max Manlove, a military policeman, reported that at 1:30 a.m. on March 7, an orange-colored, teardrop-shaped object dropped from the sky right in front of him. Visible only for a couple of seconds, the thing disappeared. But other soldiers said they saw it, too.

At 2 a.m. on March 8, infantrymen located a half-mile apart reported unknown lights in the sky over the bomb storage facility. One soldier said he saw a whitish light, and another GI, Corporal Luke B. Sims, described a lemon-shaped, yellowish-red light that appeared to be in level flight across the secure area.

Given the ultrasensitivity of the site, the Army quickly opened an investigation.

Federal authorities in the Southwest already had their figurative antenna up due to a series of unexplained aerial sightings around Los Alamos, New Mexico, that had begun in mid-December 1948. On January 31, 1949, the special agent in charge of the FBI's San Antonio office sent a one-page memo to Director J. Edgar Hoover in Washington. The agent said representatives of Army intelligence (G-2), Office of Naval Intelligence, the Air Force's Office of Special Investigation, and the FBI had been conducting weekly intelligence conferences and had recently discussed "the matter of 'unidentified aircraft,' or 'unidentified aerial phenomena,' otherwise known as 'flying discs,' 'flying saucers,' and 'balls of fire.' " The SAC told Hoover that during the previous two months, "various sightings of unexplained phenomena" had been occurring at Los Alamos. The FBI man concluded: "Up to this time little concrete information has been obtained."

A week after the Camp Hood sightings, an Army G-2 officer readied an experiment he assumed would prove that the soldiers who reported the lights had merely been seeing flares connected to routine nighttime maneuvers at the post.

Captain Horace McCulloch, assistant G-2 for the 2nd Armored Division, intended to set off a series of flares to support his hypothesis. He stationed artillery observers at key points to report by radio what the flares looked like from various distances and angles. But before the experiment began, at 7:52 p.m. on March 17, the well-trained observers reported a series of white, red, and green lights that appeared to be flying in straight lines. No one had shot any flares yet. The captain reported the incident, which included seven separate sightings, and continued with more witness interviews.

Meanwhile, the mysterious sightings over the post continued.

While on patrol at 11:50 p.m. on March 31, Lieutenant Frederick Davis observed what he described as a reddish-white fireball pass over the airstrip adjacent to the weapons storage site. When he used his field telephone to report the sighting, something caused interference on the frequency. He later estimated that the fast-moving object, traveling on a horizontal plane, traversed the field inside fifteen seconds.

G-2 had been sending its reports on the unknown aerial activity at Killeen Base to the Air Force, but that branch of the military was preoccupied with the situation at Los Alamos. When the Army heard nothing back from the Air Force, it assumed its investigators were not interested in the Camp Hood situation.

But when the sightings above the military post continued—climaxed by virtually the entire garrison seeing a formation of lights pass overhead during retreat—the base commander decided to take decisive action. He would go proactive and see if he could get to the bottom of the mystery. The general's staff quickly developed a plan: Special four-man squads equipped with sighting apparatuses designed for artillery fire control would be positioned at selected points affording the best view across the secret facility. Operating on a special radio frequency, if a team saw an aerial anomaly, it would transmit the object's azimuth angle and elevation to a command post. If multiple teams saw the object, the data could be triangulated for a fairly accurate reading of the object's direction and speed.

As preparation for the exercise continued, so did the sightings. On the night of April 27, 1949, two Camp Hood soldiers reported seeing a round, "large dull violet object...heading West." The light flashed off and on at intervals and remained visible for about a minute. In the conclusion section of the report, the sighting was listed as "Other (BIRDS)."

Though the Camp Hood sightings all occurred at night, three officers viewed an unknown aerial object at El Paso's Fort Bliss at 11:40 a.m. on May 5. Majors Charles D. May and Jones Olhausen, along with Captain Malloy C. Vaughn, reported seeing a white, oblong object traveling from west to east across the military reservation. The object reflected light, appeared to be traveling 200 to 250 miles an hour, and looked to be about the size of a three-inch disc held at arm's length. At an altitude of about 1,000 feet, it flew threw a field of practice artillery fire unscathed and remained visible for thirty to fifty seconds.

The Army Investigates Killeen Happenings

By late summer, the Army had a far more tangible threat to worry about other than mysterious lights in the night sky over Fort Bliss, Camp Hood, or New Mexico. On August 29, 1949, the Soviet Union exploded its first atomic bomb. The United States no longer enjoyed a nuclear monopoly.

A shocked citizenry read about the successful Russian nuclear test in their newspapers or heard about it on radio or television, but years would go by before the American public got any inkling that something unusual had been happening at domestic military instillations in Texas and New Mexico. In fact, the details of what happened at Camp Hood that spring did not surface publicly until 1956, when former Air Force Captain Edward J. Ruppelt published his now classic book, *The Report on Unidentified Flying Objects.* Even then, Ruppelt would only say that the perplexing rash of UFO sightings in the spring of 1949 had occurred at "a highly secret area that can't be named." He did reveal that the sightings involved the Army, and from his description of events, it is plain that he was referring to the nuclear arsenal at Killeen Base.

"The series of incidents started when military patrols…protecting the area began to report seeing formations of lights flying through the night sky," the former captain wrote. "At first the lights were reported every three or four nights, but inside of two weeks the frequency had stepped up. Before long they were a nightly occurrence. Some patrols reported that they had seen three or four formations in one night."

Having learned of the Fort Hood wave from an Army major stationed at the Pentagon who had been involved in his service's investigation of the sightings, Ruppelt said that while the description of the lights varied, "the majority of the observers reported a V formation of three lights."

The former captain continued: "As the formation moved through the sky, the lights changed in color from a bluish white to orange and back to bluish white. This color cycle took about two seconds. The lights usually traveled from west to east and made no sound. They didn't streak across the sky like a meteor, but they were 'going faster than a jet'… [and] were 'a little bigger than the biggest star.' Once in a while the GIs would get binoculars on them but they couldn't see any more details. The lights just looked bigger."

Ruppelt went on to explain how the Army had intended to investigate the Camp Hood sightings:

> When one sighting team spotted a UFO the radio operator would call out his team's location, the location of the UFO…, and the direction it was going. All of the other teams…would thus know when to look for the UFO and begin to sight on it. While the radio man was reporting, the instrument man…would line up the UFO and…call out the angles of elevation and azimuth. The timer would call out the time; the recorder would write all of this down. The command post, upon hearing the report of the UFO, would call the next patrol and tell them.

To Ruppelt's way of thinking, the operation would have been "an excellent opportunity to get some concrete data on at least one type of UFO." Observation without instrument measurement, he continued, was "miserably inaccurate."

However, he went on, "if you could accurately establish that some type of object was traveling 30,000 miles an hour—or even 3,000 miles an hour—through our atmosphere, the UFO story would be the biggest story since the Creation."

Seemingly foolproof, the Army plan was written as a field order, signed by the right people, and mimeographed for distribution to the appropriate personnel.

"Since the Air Force had the prime responsibility for the UFO investigation," Ruppelt wrote, "it was decided that the plan should be quickly coordinated with the Air Force, so a copy was rushed to them. Time was critical because every group of nightly reports might be the last. Everything was ready to roll the minute the Air Force said 'Go.' "

Street view of Fort Hood

But for reasons Ruppelt never learned, the Air Force nixed the Army's Camp Hood UFO plan. He speculated the Army operation got shot down because power was shifting among the top brass away from officers inclined to entertain extraterrestrial notions. "They [UFOs] didn't exist, they couldn't exist...Any further investigation by the Army would be a waste of time and effort."

Among converts to the extraterrestrial hypothesis were some members of the Project Sign team, who carried out the

Air Force's first formal UFO investigations. In a concluding report written in the summer of 1948, the team posited that UFOs were for real, not Russian in origin. According to Ruppelt, this finding was sent to the Pentagon but ultimately ordered destroyed by General Hoyt Vandenberg, Air Force chief of staff, on the basis that no conclusive evidence had been offered to support that view.

Judging from Project Blue Book reports released under the Federal Freedom of Information Act, the post commander at Hood decided to proceed with a coordinated UFO tracking effort despite the lack of buy-in from the Air Force. On the night of May 6, two days after the system had been activated, artillery observers spotted an unidentified aerial object over the camp. At 7:40 p.m. the following day, observers tracked another UFO over the base. Lieutenant Mardell Ward noted a diamond-shaped object at 1,000 feet, moving to the northwest. The bright white light remained visible for fifty-seven seconds and was estimated as traveling at 1,300 miles an hour. On May 8, Ward and two other observers recorded another sighting, this one beginning at 10:08 p.m. and continuing for nine minutes. The object looked like the one seen the night before, though this time its altitude was estimated at 1,600 feet. But on this night, Ward reported something different: Severe radio interference that ended once the object was no longer visible.

The final recorded sighting occurred at 9:05 p.m. on June 6. Several observers saw an orange object that appeared to be thirty to seventy feet in diameter hovering a mile above ground three miles south of the observation post and four and a half miles south of the plotting center. The object remained visible for nearly three minutes before moving horizontally and exploding. If any debris was found on the ground, it went unreported.

Though no further effort would be made to determine the nature of the lights that had been buzzing the secret nuclear weapons facility in Texas, the Air Force began its most ambitious UFO investigation in early 1952 with the launching of Project Blue Book. A World War II veteran, Ruppelt got the nod as the project's director.

Two Decades Later

Twenty years after the still-unexplained wave of Fort Hood UFO sightings, the Army shut down Killeen Base and removed all nuclear weapons. The facility was transferred to Fort Hood's administration and in August 1969 became the headquarters for the Army testing of night vision equipment. The Army's first assault helicopter company was assigned to assist in the training mission.

The increase in night flying those changes stimulated led to another round of UFO sightings, but by this time Project Blue Book had ended and the general conclusion was that any mysterious lights seen at night in the area had to do with helicopters and night vision experimentation—not visitors from another universe.

In 1989, a soldier stationed at Fort Hood told his superiors he had seen a large cylindrical-shaped object float across the base during daytime training exercises. At the same time, he said, the base experienced power outages. Security personnel interviewed him, but the matter apparently ended with that.

The former Q Area is now known as West Fort Hood and the former Gray Air Force Base is now operated by the Army. Throughout the presidency of George W. Bush, Air Force One often landed at the former Air Force base when the president and his wife returned to Texas to spend some time at their ranch near Crawford.

Following the terrorist attacks of September 11, 2001, and the beginning of the subsequent two-fronted war in Afghanistan and Iraq, and given that Fort Hood is the nation's largest military installation, the airspace over this part of the state was restricted and closely monitored. But at 9:30 p.m. on

August 2, 2007, three witnesses saw two strange objects in the sky in the vicinity of the fort.

"My husband was standing in our front yard talking to a friend of his," the woman said. "He came in to get me and told me to check it out. I looked up and there was something flying extremely fast. About a minute later another one followed."

Living near the fort, the couple was used to seeing military aircraft, but they had never seen anything like the object they observed that summer night.

"We have watched the space station go over us numerous times," the woman continued, "and these things moved a lot faster than that. There were no flashing lights, just a steady white-like glow."

Chapter 7:
"Damn...look at those lights!"
Lubbock, 1951

Texas Technological College sophomore Kenneth Davis pulled his car up next to the speaker stand at the Corral Drive-In Theater on the Idalou Highway and attached the heavy metal amplifier to the door on the driver's side.

It had been a hot day, but one of Lubbock's saving graces is that it stands on the high plains of the Llano Estacado, 3,202 feet above sea level. Even in summer, when the sun heads down, a low-humidity day fades into a nicely cool evening. In the small Bell County community of Holland where Davis grew up, humidity would make the August heat linger all night long.

As Davis tried to divide his attention between the action on the big screen and the pretty co-ed sitting next to him, something else caught his eye. Appearing low on the horizon and seemingly coming from the direction of Floydada, a V-shaped formation of pale yellow lights moved rapidly across the moonless sky.

"It was a large V, more than the wingspan of a [Boeing] 747, moving at a heroic rate of speed," Davis later recalled of that night in 1951.

His date also noticed the lights, leaning over Davis to look out the window on his side of the car. "That was not at all unpleasant," Davis smiled decades later. "Our cheeks touched."

Elsewhere in Lubbock, Texas Tech petroleum engineering professor W.L. Ducker happened to look skyward.

"Damn," he blurted, "look at those lights."

His two companions that night, Dr. A.G. Oberg, a professor of chemical engineering, and Dr. W.I. Robinson, a geology professor, turned their heads upward and saw the same thing: A fast-moving formation of lights.

Ducker looked at his watch: 9:20 p.m.

The three friends had gathered at Robinson's house that Saturday night for an evening of free-ranging conversation. They met like this periodically, their only rule being no discussion of politics. Tonight's topic loosely centered on astronomy while they watched the heavens for meteors. The professors sat in metal lawn chairs in Robinson's back yard. They had arranged the chairs so that each person sat facing a different direction, but placed them close enough together for ease of communication. Oberg and Robinson puffed on their pipes as they looked up at the stars. None of them was drinking, and they never did, unless they sipped iced tea. On this night, Robinson had forgotten to make any.

The lights first appeared in the northeast sky and traveled on a straight path to the southwest. They looked to be very high and fast moving. Having seen something far more unusual than shooting stars, the three scientists began an animated discussion of what it had been.

Back at the drive-in on the east side of town, when the lights above disappeared, Davis and his date returned their attention to the movie—and each other. But an hour-and-a-half later (though some witnesses said less time passed by), the formation of lights reappeared, this time heading in the opposite direction. Again, Davis and his companion watched them until they disappeared.

The three professors, still talking about what they had seen earlier, were amazed to see the lights a second time.

"We felt no shock waves such as an object traveling at such a high speed in the lower atmosphere would give off," Ducker later told a reporter. "The absence of such shock waves would indicate that the formation was flying in the stratosphere, 50,000 feet or higher."

People all across Lubbock, then a city of 75,000, also saw the lights that night. But they saw them differently. To Davis and his girlfriend, the lights amounted to little more than a curiosity, something they had never seen before. Neither had any idea what they were.

But the three PhDs were scientists, trained to be observant but not to jump to conclusions without sufficient data to support a hypothesis. They viewed the lights with professional interest.

Still, despite their collective knowledge, without any reference point in the sky, they had no way of calculating the size of the objects, their speed, or their altitude. All they could do was guess. First, they concluded the lights had only been visible for three seconds, crossing from horizon to horizon within that fleeting time frame. They appeared "electric blue" in color and twinkled. Next, the men agreed the objects must have been at least nine miles high and traveling at 18,000 miles an hour—covering thirty degrees per second.

Between them, the three professors had plenty of life experience, but none of them had ever seen anything like what they observed that Saturday night.

"Frankly, we were astonished," Ducker later admitted. "If I had not had confirming witnesses at the time I feel sure I should have said nothing about what I saw, for it is incredible to believe they are of terrestrial origin and even more incredible to believe they are from beyond the earth."

Carl Hart Takes Some Pictures
Five days later, 18-year-old Tech freshman Carl Hart, Jr., who lived on 19th Street not far from the college campus,

moved his bed next to a window in the hope of catching some breeze on an unusually hot night. It was 11:30 p.m. on Thursday, August 30, 1951. As he lay looking out at the stars, a set of fast-moving lights appeared suddenly in the sky. They formed a V.

Hart jumped out of bed and grabbed his camera, an inexpensive 35 mm Kodak. Setting the aperture at f3.5—nearly wide open—he adjusted the exposure to a tenth of a second and ran outside.

Though the formation had disappeared, the lights soon made another pass over the city. He braced the camera as well as he could and shot three frames before the lights again moved out of view. When the lights showed up a third time, he snapped two more exposures.

"There were three flights and I got pictures of the last two," Hart later recalled. "Took two of one flight and three of the other."

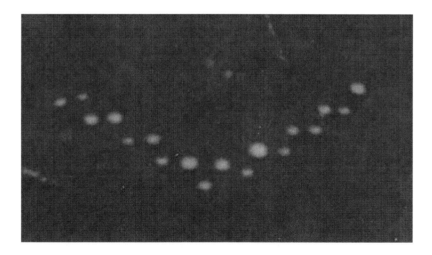

In the morning, Hart called a friend who had a photography lab and got him to develop the film from the night before. As the images slowly materialized in the developing tray, the two young men saw a blurry, V-shaped set of white spots come into view against the black background of the sky. When the photos had been washed and dried, at the suggestion of his friend, Hart took the black and white prints to the city's daily newspaper, the *Avalanche-Journal*.

Long-time editor Charlie Guy was more than happy to publish them. Hart had not even asked for any money for the pictures, which ran on page one of the morning edition of Saturday, September 1. "Mysterious Objects in Lubbock Sky," the photo caption began. "It's anybody's guess what they are, but the mysterious objects in the photos above are believed to be the 'thing' which Lubbockites have been seeing in the sky during recent nights."

A twenty-two-paragraph story by reporter Kenneth May, "Flying 'Whatsits' Seen Again," accompanied the photographs. Indeed, the lights had over flown the city once more on Friday night, sightings reported from 8:40 to 10:37 p.m. The newspaper, known locally as the A-J, received numerous telephone calls from residents who said they had seen the mystery lights. The police department and local radio stations also got a lot of calls.

"All those reporting the objects described them as flying in a V-shaped or U-shaped formations and passing through the sky almost directly overhead within from 3 to 7 seconds," the newspaper reported. "The number of 'dots' reported in the formation ranged from eight or nine to '20 or 30.' "

Reporter May wrote that Dr. J.C. Cross, head of Tech's biology department, had taken a look at Hart's photographs and could come up with no suggestion as to what they were. But he did make one assertion: "It definitely wasn't caused by birds."

Witnesses interviewed by May all agreed the objects had been traveling far faster than birds could fly. "They were flying faster than any jet plane I ever saw," Hart offered.

May also contacted Reese Air Force Base, a pilot training facility established six miles west of town during World War II and reactivated in 1948, and asked if the base had any aircraft flying that night. An Air Force officer said "to our knowledge," no aircraft had been up. The Civil Aeronautics Administration (predecessor of the Federal Aviation Administration) office at Lubbock Municipal Airport said no civilian aircraft had been passing over the city at the time of the light sightings.

The newspaper made Hart's images available to the wire services, which distributed them worldwide. Hundreds of newspapers ran the pictures, and the self-styled Hub City of the Plains got more free publicity over the next several days than the Chamber of Commerce could ever have hoped to achieve through brochures or paid advertising.

Meanwhile, the nighttime light show over Lubbock continued.

At 9:20 p.m. on September 13, Dr. R.S. Underwood, chairman of the mathematics department at Tech, saw the lights along with his wife and three friends. The formation appeared to pass right over his house at 2220 Broadway, between downtown and the college campus. The professor's father-in-law also saw the lights. Underwood later wrote that knowing the locations of these witnesses gave him sufficient data to calculate the altitude and speed of the lights. They had been 2,100 feet in the air traveling 750 miles an hour, he concluded.

Project Blue Book

Later that month, Air Force Captain Edward J. Ruppelt sat down at his desk at Wright Patterson Air Force Base outside Dayton, Ohio. The World War II veteran coordinated Project Blue Book, his service's ongoing investigation into UFO phenomenon. Through Project Blue Book and a series of earlier initiatives, the Air Force kept tabs on the Cold War UFO wave that started with a sighting by pilot Kenneth Arnold over the Cascade Mountains in Washington State on June 24,

1947. Soon, the young woman in charge of delivering the mail placed a stack of letters in the officer's in-box.

One of the pieces came from Reese Air Force Base in Lubbock. The envelop contained a lengthy report from the facility's intelligence officer on the ongoing sightings occurring in that part of Texas as well as newspaper clippings, including the story illustrated with Hart's photographs. Another letter contained a report of a UFO sighting near Kirtland Air Force Base in Albuquerque, New Mexico. The witness was an employee of the nuclear weapon testing facility in the Sandia Mountains, a man with a top security clearance. The man's wife had also seen what they described as a giant "flying wing." That had occurred about dusk on the night of August 25, only twenty minutes before the multiple sightings in Lubbock, 250 miles distant. The last piece of mail contained the report of an unidentified fast-moving radar contact at 13,000 feet over Washington State in the early morning hours of August 26, an incident which had prompted the scrambling of an interceptor jet. Before the fighter pilot reached that altitude, the contact disappeared from the scope.

Ruppelt took a map of the United States and saw that a near-straight line could be drawn from Lubbock through Albuquerque to the point of the radar contact in the northwest. A superfast-moving object or objects could easily have covered that distance on the same night.

First, the captain sent a set of the Lubbock photographs to the intelligence officer at Kirtland AFB so he could show the images to the Albuquerque witnesses. When he got a Teletype from Kirtland that the witness said the Lubbock photos looked like what he and his wife had seen, Ruppelt made reservations for a commercial flight to Lubbock, where an Office of Special Investigations (OSI) officer at Reese already had a meeting scheduled with the professors. After reaching Lubbock, Ruppelt was taken to meet with the four men. They talked well into the night as the scientists methodically set forth their observations and the conclusions they had drawn from them.

Returning to the visiting officer's quarters at Reese early the following morning, Ruppelt stayed up for several hours more pondering all that he had heard. Finally turning in, he managed a few hours sleep. Later that morning, his first full day in Lubbock, Ruppelt was escorted by the OSI officer to meet with Hart to discuss his photographs.

He got Hart to reenact how he had taken the photos and then borrowed the negatives for detailed analysis.

Ruppelt rounded out his Lubbock trip by talking with other people who had witnesses the lights, including an elderly rancher at Lamesa who thought they were migrating plover. Meanwhile, as Ruppelt worked to complete his report, two OSI agents drove to Matador, seventy miles northeast of Lubbock, to interview a woman and her daughter who said they had seen a metallic pear-shaped object the day same as the Lubbock sightings. The investigators did a discreet background check on the women and were convinced they were not making up their story.

On his return flight from Lubbock to Dallas, the captain met a man who did not know he was in charge of the Air Force's UFO investigation. Comfortable in confiding with a total stranger, the man told Ruppelt how his wife had been scared half to death after seeing a strange aerial object over their ranch near Lubbock. He, too, described the object as a flying wing with flashing blue lights that moved silently overhead. Fearing people would think he and his wife were crazy, he had not reported the incident, which he said occurred about ten minutes prior to the time the professors and others saw the lights in Lubbock. Since the Albuquerque sighting and what the two women had seen near Matador was known only by the military and had not been publicly reported, the man's story "hit me right between the eyes," Ruppelt later admitted.

Back in Ohio, Ruppelt had the negatives examined by photography experts who concluded they seemed to be genuine. However, an effort to produce similar images of aerial lights at night proved unsuccessful. The officer's voluminous report eventually concluded the Lubbock lights were birds.

Life magazine with a cover story about flying saucers

More National Exposure

The lights continued to appear periodically through November, but then they stopped. By spring, while many of those who had seen the aerial formations—especially the college professors—had definitely not forgotten them, the matter had dropped off the public's figurative radar screen. But when the April 7, 1952, issue of *Life* hit the newsstands and arrived in subscribers' mailboxes, Lubbock residents found more in the weekly news magazine to be interested in than the black and white cover photograph of a bare-shouldered young blonde named Marilyn Monroe. "There Is A Case For Interplanetary Saucers" read the headline just to the upper right of the starlet's curls. Of ten compelling incidents offered in support of the possibility that Earth was being visited from outer space, the Lubbock Lights ranked number one.

"The Lubbock Lights, flying in formation, are considered by the Air Force the most unexplainable phenomena yet observed," the article pronounced. The spread featured two of Hart's photographs, a mug shot of the crew-cut student photographer, and a group photo showing Tech professors Oberg, Ducker, Robinson, and George. Following an overview of the August 1951 sightings, the article's authors began an evaluation of the Lubbock case with this: "The observations have been too numerous and too similar to be doubted. In addition the Air Force, after the closest examination, has found nothing fraudulent about Hart's pictures. The lights are much too bright to be reflections, and therefore bodies containing sources of light."

After the magazine came out, the four professors wrote a letter to the editor saying that they did not believe Hart's pictures had captured the phenomenon they witnessed. To that assertion, the magazine replied: "Air Force experts had considered these objections of Professor Ducker and Doctors Oberg, Robinson and George. But they are still convinced that Hart was able to get exposures of the two groups he saw (four seconds for each to cross the sky, one to one-and-a-half minutes apart) and found no reason to repudiate his pictures."

In its June 9, 1952, issue, *Time* magazine weighed in with a flying saucer story that made brief mention of the Lubbock Lights. This story, based on an interview with Dr. Donald H. Menzel, associate director of solar research at Harvard, said all

UFO sightings could be attributed to natural phenomenon or hoaxes. Flying saucers, Menzel said, "are as real as rainbows. No one should be ashamed of seeing them and reporting them. I have seen them myself." But, the article continued, "seeing flying saucers is not the same thing as believing that they are spaceships manned by intelligent beings from another planet." (*Life*'s weekly rival, *Look,* also ran a UFO-debunking story that week quoting Menzel in somewhat more detail on the Lubbock Lights.)

Reported sightings of lights in the night sky, such as occurred at Lubbock, were merely mirages caused by reflected light bouncing off temperature inversions, Menzel declared in so many words.

"I don't believe what I saw was a reflection from streetlights," Tech's Dr. George told the *Avalanche-Journal* after the *Look* story came out. Faculty colleague Ducker added: "All we can say about what we saw is how they acted, not what they were."

Tech Prof Does His Own Investigation

That fall, Ducker decided to conduct his own investigation into the Lubbock lights. Wondering if the lights would appear again as fall approached, the petroleum engineer undertook a home electronics project and built a highly sensitive microphone. If the objects did show back up, he wanted to know if they made any sounds, be it the honking of geese or a high-atmosphere sonic boom.

In September 1952, the lights did reappear over Lubbock. But Ducker's electronic big ear, which could easily amplify distant conversations, heard nothing as the formation passed overhead.

While not picking anything up on his microphone, Ducker got a good enough look at the lights to note that when they disappeared, they did not fade out. Rather, they vanished instantly, "as if something had turned them off," as he later recalled. He still wondered if the dots in the sky were created by light from below reflecting off whatever the objects were.

Thinking the city's fairly new mercury-vapor street light system might be the culprit, he designed an experiment to prove or disprove his theory. Talking the local weather bureau out of one of its observation balloons, Ducker attached a series of white napkins to the helium-filled bag and observed the balloon through high-powered binoculars at specific heights as it ascended. At about three hundred feet, one of the napkins reflected light from below.

But as Ducker later admitted, that did not prove the phenomenon had been caused by light reflecting off migratory birds, as his colleagues and others had come to suspect. All it really demonstrated was that the streetlights were bouncing light rays from an airborne object. So he tried another experiment. The next time he saw the mystery lights, he threw a powerful beam from a borrowed searchlight into the sky. At first he saw nothing, but then he could make out webbed feet in the formation. He concluded the lights were caused by reflection from birds and reported his findings to the Air Force.

In his 1956 book, *The Report on Unidentified Flying Objects,* Ruppelt changed his mind about the lights being birds. He wrote:

"They weren't birds, they weren't refracted light, but they weren't spaceships. The lights that the professors saw—the backbone of the Lubbock Light series—have been positively identified as a very commonplace and easily explainable natural phenomenon."

But compounding mystery with mystery, Ruppelt said he could not divulge who had come up with the explanation or how.

On the 20th anniversary of the mysterious sightings, *Avalanche-Journal* reporter Gerry Burton interviewed the major players of two decades before.

Oberg told Burton that he and his two Tech colleagues ultimately "decided it was birds fluorescing in the bright lights on 19th Street..." and lamented having "made the mistake of telling about the lights" and wondered if he would ever "live it down."

Another of the professors, Robinson, said he "got...disgusted with the whole business" and declined to discuss the event other than to note that the "officials investigating the lights" had not viewed him or the other two faculty members as crackpots. Despite the passage of two decades, he continued, he still received mail from people wanting to know about the lights, particularly from students. "I think they just want me to write them a theme," he laughed.

Professor Ducker, always the more willing to talk, told Burton that while he also had tried to avoid publicity, he had not stopped thinking about the lights. Despite his 1952 experiment that led him to his bird theory, he remained open minded about the origin of the lights.

"We have a tendency to say such and such is impossible when we should say that there is no way, in the light of present scientific knowledge, for it to be possible," he said.

Hart, still living in Lubbock, told Burton he did not buy the Air Force's conclusion that the lights had been caused by migrating birds.

"I really don't know what it was," he said, "but if it had been birds there would have been some sound. You can hear birds. There was no sound."

The Air Force eventually returned his negatives, Hart said. Over the years, he lost two of them, but he placed the other three in a safe deposit box. Looking back on how those hastily snapped images affected his life, he said: "It was a lot of fun at first, but it got to be kind of a nuisance."

In 1977, a Phoenix-based group called Ground Saucer Watch used a computer to analyze Hart's images. Though the organization had exposed other UFO photographs as "clever hoaxes" the group pronounced the Lubbock shots as "a formation of extraordinary flying objects." While stressing that it was only commenting on the photographs, not the reports of witnesses, one researcher for the group said, "The image in each exposure are not airplanes, astronomical bodies, nor birds flying low to the ground and being illuminated by mercury-vapor street lights."

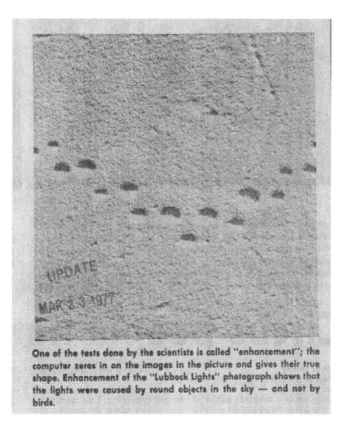

One of the tests done by the scientists is called "enhancement"; the computer zeros in on the images in the picture and gives their true shape. Enhancement of the "Lubbock Lights" photograph shows that the lights were caused by round objects in the sky — and not by birds.

When Lubbock celebrated its centennial as an incorporated city in 2009, the *Avalanche-Journal* did yet another retrospective on the "Flying Whatsits." The article broke no new ground, but did put the 1951 incident into nicely metaphorical perspective: "More than 50 years later, the mysterious 'Lubbock Lights' have faded into little more than a dark mystery and celebrated UFO case illuminated mostly by conjecture, speculation and a few photographs."

In the final analysis, Captain Ruppelt penned the most incontrovertible statement on the case in his book about Project Blue Book: "Although the case of the Lubbock Lights is officially dead, its memory lingers on."

CHAPTER 8:
MILITARY PILOTS SAW THEM, TOO:
LAREDO AND GALVESTON: 1952

Airfields proliferated like jackrabbits across the Texas landscape during World War II. Many met their demise after the war, but twenty-eight Air Force bases remained active in the Lone Star State through the 1950s. Aircraft of all kinds buzzed over large cities and humble towns. San Antonio's four bases made it a regular military hub, and practically every West Texas burg of any size boasted a military contingent. Jets even soared over the lonely sand dunes of Monahans. Some of the bases helped secure important American assets, like the Houston ship channel, while isolated spots like Matagorda Island served as bombing ranges.

Political clout did not hurt the state's military fortunes; two of the era's most powerful federal politicians hailed from Texas. Bonham's own Sam Rayburn was in the midst of a nearly seventeen-year run as speaker of the House, and future president Lyndon B. Johnson had begun building his political power base as the Senate's minority whip.

Meanwhile, flying saucers became imprinted on the American psyche and cinema. Alien craft zipped across movie screens almost weekly in the 1950s.

Two decades later, UFOlogist William H. Spaulding used Freedom of Information Act requests to mine government records in search of clues to their origins. His research led him

111

to the conclusion that UFO sightings most commonly occurred within a hundred miles of military proving grounds. Also, spikes often followed tense events such as Sputnik's launch in 1957, he noted.

Dr. Edward Uhler Condon disagreed. He read classified reports a decade earlier than Spaulding and considered such analysis unproven and sensational. Few people carried more weight in the scientific study of UFOs than Condon. Bowing to Congressional pressure in 1966, the Air Force contracted with the University of Colorado to conduct an eighteen-month UFO study. They put Condon in charge. The respected scientist and radar expert had worked on the development of the atomic bomb and survived an attack by the House Un-American Activities Committee with his credibility intact.

Condon found no statistically significant evidence that people see UFOs more often near military installations. Instead he noted in his official 1969 summary that "geographical distribution of reports correlates roughly with population density in nonurban areas." In other words, strange things in the sky are easier to see without the clutter of city lights, and they are more likely to be spotted where lots of people live in the country.

Spaulding's theory and Condon's may be at odds, but both men would seemingly agree on one thing: Texas was prime UFO territory in the 1950s.

Interest and Disinterest

The early 1950s offered up all the ingredients for a juicy smorgasbord of UFO stories, but top Air Force leaders did want to taste the buffet. However, they were sensitive to the effects of UFO reports on the public and began to lift a few veils of secrecy to allay worries about invading terrestrial or extraterrestrial forces.

For example, the Navy announced in February 1951 that all reliable flying saucer reports made in the previous three-

and-half years could be attributed to plastic balloons it floated 100,000 feet into the atmosphere to study cosmic rays. The lighted bottoms of these "skyhook" balloons could easily be mistaken for flying saucers, particularly at dawn or dusk, according to Dr. Urner Liddel, chief nuclear physicist for the Office of Naval Research. The balloons had been kept secret under national security guidelines until the 1951 announcement, Liddle told the press.

And eight months later, the Air Force hoped to avoid confusion by announcing in advance plans to release high altitude balloons on the East and West costs to study wind currents, following successful tests at Holloman Air Force Base in Alamogordo, New Mexico.

But in 1949, nonbelievers held the reigns of power. The Air Force announced on December 27 plans to close Project Grudge, its flying-saucer investigation mission. One or two lonely officers at Ohio's Wright-Patterson Air Force Base continued logging the few reports that trickled in, but underlings well understood that expressing belief in—or even open mindedness about—flying saucers could be hazardous to military careers, according to Captain Edward J. Ruppelt's memoirs.

Ruppelt took over Project Grudge in late 1951. A sighting by military pilots and radar operators over New Jersey in September of that year focused new Air Force attention on unexplained phenomena. Investigators ultimately determined that a flustered student radar operator conducting a demonstration for higher-ups excitedly and mistakenly exclaimed that a low-altitude target moved too fast for his set to register. In fact, the student had not followed proper procedures for switching to automatic tracking and mistook a conventional 400-mile-an-hour airplane for a flying saucer. But in the months it took to figure that out, a group of colonels and generals became concerned that Project Grudge had not investigated sightings as vigorously as they assumed.

When Ruppelt inherited the languishing project, he added more staff and standardized reporting procedures. The powers that were backed him up by ordering that all military UFO sightings be reported to Ruppelt's team. The captain considered lack of objectivity grounds for dismissal from that team. He also is generally credited with coining the term "unidentified flying object," deeming "flying saucer" too specific and presumptuous.

Official military interest in flying saucers may have waned in the last days of the 1940s, but public interest did not. In the absence of official information, investigative reporters began digging around for themselves. One of them was Donald Keyhoe, a retired Marine major who sometimes wrote for the men's magazine *True*. Its editor turned to him for help with a flying saucer article in 1949.

The Air Force brass dismissed Keyhoe when he came knocking. This snub did not cover up secrets, Ruppelt contended. Leadership just did not want to waste time on a subject they deemed frivolous. Even a couple of Keyhoe's Annapolis classmates, by then Navy admirals, could not provide him any useful information.

This lack of military response helped convince Keyhoe and his editor (who apparently did not need much convincing) that spacecraft from other worlds routinely visited ours. The military knew this, they reasoned, but authorities denied and withheld such knowledge to avoid public panic. Keyhoe's article, "Flying Saucers Are Real," caused a huge sensation when *True* published it in the January 1950 issue. He quickly expanded the story into a hot-selling paperback.

The New Jersey incident prompted dozens of other well-respected publications to renew their interest in flying saucers. Magazines such as *Newsweek*, *Time*, the *New Yorker*, and *Popular Science* helped make 1952 a record year for UFO sightings.

The article that most concerned the Air Force appeared in April of that year in the venerable pages of *Life*. Most reporters who inquired about UFOs seemed content with the "hoaxes, hallucinations, and misidentifications" line, or at least they did not press the military very hard for more specific explanations. *Life* reporter Bob Ginna, however, wanted to hear it from the horse's mouth. He notified the Air Force that he planned to visit Wright-Patterson and talk directly to the folks doing the investigating. Air Force officials scrambled anxiously to pull the files Ginna requested, an observation not lost on the reporter, Ruppelt recalled.

Ginna's article leant credence to the notion of extraterrestrial visitors by attributing it to high-ranking Air Force officials. Most of the top brass did not buy the ET theory, but a few who believed it sat so high up on the chain of command that their personal opinions carried the weight of policy, Ruppelt explained.

By the time the *Life* article hit the newsstands, hundreds of newspapers had teased it. Coincidentally, the Air Force issued a press release the same week announcing that Project Grudge would be henceforth be called Project Blue Book. The deluge of UFO reports duly intensified.

UFO Zeitgeist

Clearly, serious people took UFOs seriously in the early 1950s, among them Carl Jung. The influential Swiss psychiatrist began writing letters and papers on the topic in the early 1950s. If flying saucers were not physical realities, Jung theorized, they were projections from the collective unconscious.

"At a time when the world is divided by an iron curtain—a fact unheard-of in human history—we might expect all sorts of funny things, since when such a thing happens in an individual it means a complete disassociation, which is instantly compensated by symbols of wholeness and unity," Jung wrote to an American friend in February 1951. "It's just too bad that we don't know enough about it."

By the end of the decade, Jung would publicly deny personal belief in flying saucers, concluding that they were products of human desire for a "new savior myth."

The Flap of '52

Be they physical or psychic, plenty of people kept on the look out for UFOs. As the Air Force's investigative activities enjoyed a new lease on life, so did the Ground Observer Corp (GOC), a wartime organization revived in the early 1950s. At its peak during World War II, the GOC coordinated the activities of 1.5 million civilian observers watching American coastlines for German and Japanese aircraft.

Like Project Grudge, the GOC got a new name in 1952—Operation Skywatch. Radar of the day could not detect low-flying aircraft, the Air Force explained, so the job of warning the military of a stealth Russian invasion could conceivably fall to civilians with binoculars. More than 750,000 patriots watched the skies in shifts at some 16,000 posts. On July 14, the Air Force called for round-the-clock activation of these volunteers.

The military acknowledged that it too had been watching the skies closely since before fighting began in Korea. By 1952, the Air Force maintained a "continuous state of readiness" along the nation's coasts and boarders and near all vital industrial and military installations, according to news reports from the time.

The most spectacular UFO sightings of a very busy July began the weekend after Operation Skywatch's name officially changed. On two consecutive Saturday nights, radar operators and airline pilots reported lights behaving strangely in restricted air space over the nation's capital. The interlopers would disappear or shoot away when military jets tried to intercept them, then reappear after the pilots gave up and

116

headed back to their bases. Finally, at 3:20 a.m. on July 27, Lieutenant William Patterson got a closer look. He claimed a giant ring of blue-white lights briefly surrounded his aircraft.

Despite Lieutenant Patterson's dramatic description and the skepticism of radar operators on duty during the sightings, authorities dismissed the anomalies as temperature inversions that bent light and deflected radar signals in strange ways. Columns of cold air that break through warm layers can particularly confuse radar systems, the Civil Aeronautics Administration (CAA) reported months later. However, Ruppelt felt conducting a more rigorous investigation and sharing the results with the public could have diffused the UFO frenzy.

With Americans on alert and sensitized to UFOS, sightings peaked that summer. CIA officials speculated that a national case of "midsummer madness" might have taken hold. Overall, 1,501 UFOs were reported in 1952, and 20 percent would ultimately remain unexplained.

Texans naturally contributed their share, including:

July 3—The news editor of the *Hugo Daily News*, an Oklahoma paper published just across the Red River from Paris, Texas, reported that he and fifteen other Army reserve officers undergoing training at Fort Hood watched two flying saucers traveling at "tremendous speeds."

July 18—A Uvalde witness reported to Project Blue Book the sighting of "a large, round, silver object that spun on its vertical axis."

July 31—The Galveston *Daily News*, which published UFO stories more liberally than some papers, printed an editorial lamenting an up tick in local sightings of a speedy craft with "swept-back wings." The paper speculated that readers might be seeing Sabre jets. "Perhaps there is some truth to the 'flying saucer' rumor. We don't know. But we do know that Galveston, like a few areas in the country, could become infested with a flood of 'saucer' reports. We hope that does not happen and people exercise caution in hysterical reports to authorities."

August 2—Harry O. Stanley of Hitchcock told the Galveston *Daily News* of being startled at 1:30 a.m. by dogs barking and chickens cackling. When he went outside to investigate, he saw a round, yellow object bright enough to read by. The high-flying, fast-moving object had a streaming tail.

August 14—Captain Max M. Jacoby, chief pilot of Pioneer Airlines, and his crew chased a big, orange light near Dallas' Love Field. "It was bright, then it began to die down. I couldn't tell whether it was just a light or a light coming from some object," he told a reporter.

Keyhoe and Project Blue Book

Civilian aviators were not the only flyers trying to catch up with UFOs that year, but being fully indoctrinated in the loose-lips-sink-ships philosophy, Air Force pilots did not often discuss their experiences publicly. Because of that, most surviving accounts of military encounters come from the official reports airmen filed for Project Blue Book or from the questionable writings of Keyhoe, who quickly became one of the first UFO evangelists.

An Iowa native, Keyhoe graduated from the Naval Preparatory Academy a year after the end of World War I. An arm injury shortened his initial military career, but he re-enlisted during World War II and rose to the rank of major in the Naval Aviation Training Division.

Keyhoe tasted the power of promotion when he managed a successful national tour for Charles Lindbergh in 1927. A year later, he published his first book, *Flying with Lindbergh*, and launched a free-lance writing career. He penned some nonfiction aviation articles in the 1920s and '30s, but Keyhoe became best known for science fiction stories published in pulp magazines such as *Weird Tales* and *Flying Aces*. His characters included military superheroes.

The success Keyhoe enjoyed from the *True* article and subsequent book set his career on a new trajectory. He presented himself in his early flying-saucer tomes as an insider and confidant to high-ranking, but often anonymous, officers. Written as breathless streams of consciousness, the books chronicled specially arranged visits to the Pentagon and quoted dialogue from cockpit conversations he could not have overheard firsthand.

Some officers may have initially encouraged or humored Keyhoe, but he would eventually become a thorn in the sides of the Air Force and CIA. From 1956 to 1969, Keyhoe led the official-sounding National Investigations Committee on Aerial Phenomena (NICAP) and used it as a platform to promote his pro-spaceman views. Several other civilian UFO groups sprang up in the 1950s.

Opinions varied as to the validity of Keyhoe's work. The octogenarian Jung felt that Keyhoe's writings "studiously avoid[ed] the wild speculations, naiveté or prejudice of other publications." On the other hand, UFO skeptic Peter Brookesmith described Keyhoe as "a freelance hack who was based in Washington, D.C., and who was struggling to make a living" before *True* published that first flying saucer article.

Views of Keyhoe also reflected a real schism in the Air Force between those who believed in extraterrestrials and those who did not. Air Force press secretary Albert M. Chop referred to Keyhoe as a "responsible, accurate reporter" in promoting the author's 1953 book, *Flying Saucers From Outer Space*. Ruppelt on the other hand sarcastically thanked Keyhoe for reading the minds of military leaders. "Keyhoe had based his conjecture on facts, and his facts were correct, even if his conjecture wasn't," the captain wrote.

Regardless of motives or voracity, Keyhoe's writing propelled him to UFO stardom. And thanks to his 1953 best seller, two Texas tales survive to this day. Several Internet sites repeat them as unassailable fact.

The events occurred just two days apart during the first week of December 1952. Stories published by Houston's daily newspapers that week reflect the paranoia of the era with almost daily coverage of the McCarthy hearings. One lengthy article described a six-engine Russian Type 31 bomber with a "swept-wing" design and a new Soviet "mother plane" that could save fuel by ferrying two MIG-15 bombers to Korea.

President Dwight D. Eisenhower visited American soldiers in Korea that week but made sure to leave behind a prefilmed newsreel to be released on the eve of Pearl Harbor Day. In it, he once again appealed for participation in Operation Skywatch.

"On this December 7, 1952, the eleventh anniversary of the surprise attack on Pearl Harbor, I will call your attention to the fact that an attack of this nature can happen again," the president said. "Because of the immense destructive power of the atomic bomb, we must maintain vigilance so that our cities and our industries will be less vulnerable to devastating attack. I therefore call upon all citizens who reside in communities which have been designated as possible enemy air approach areas to volunteer their services to this vital task."

Laredo, December 4

The first documented Texas military sighting that December occurred in Laredo, a proud border city with a long military heritage. Laredoans took their Cold War responsibilities so seriously, that in 1964 they opened an underground high school that could double as a fall-out shelter for 2,500 Rio Grande Valley residents.

Keyhoe's version of the sighting, as woven into the rambling narrative of *Flying Saucers from Outer Space*, closely tracked most of the facts documented in Project Blue Book reports. A heavy dose of assumption, along with incredibly detailed conversations between Keyhoe and a mystery pilot with whom he shared the Project Blue Book report, helped move the story along.

Keyhoe by habit changed names to protect the innocent, national security, or himself. The modern reader is never completely sure which. The Air Force apparently scrubbed the Laredo pilot's name from the documents they let Keyhoe read at the Pentagon, so the author dubbed him Lieutenant Earl Fogle. The eventually declassified report identifies the flyer as Lieutenant Robert O. Arnold.

On December 4, 1952, Lieutenant Arnold took off from Laredo Air Force Base to log required flight hours in a T-28 training aircraft (Keyhoe's version has Lieutenant Fogle flying an F-51). After a couple of hours aloft, Arnold headed back to the base only to find a queue of students pilots waiting to land.

All Arnold could do was wait, so he climbed to 6,000 feet.

After circling the base for about forty-five minutes, he looked out the cockpit window to estimate his time until landing. He counted three trainers still in the air, but then he noticed something else. A bluish light hovered at 1,500 to 2,000 feet, flying over a residential area southwest of the base. The lieutenant quickly dismissed the light as belonging to another jet, according to his official intelligence report.

Arnold made a steep left turn to get a better look at the light, which moved along a southeasterly course. As he approached, the light shot up to match his altitude and began circling the base counterclockwise at great speed. Over the next several minutes, it settled back to 1,500 feet, then flitted up swiftly to 15,000.

When the light once again matched Arnold's altitude, he headed straight toward it. The object in turn sped up and headed straight for the lieutenant's plane. This aeronautic game of chicken ended with the object passing within fifty yards of the aircraft. The official report described it as "a blurred, reddish-bluish haze of undetermined size and shape, but definitely no larger than his craft."

As the object seemed to position itself for another pass, the intelligence report says Arnold turned off his running lights out of fright and spiraled steeply left to 1,500 feet. The object then turned sharply to the right, headed south, and flitted out of sight into the stratosphere.

In novel-like dialogue between himself and a mysterious Captain Riordan, Keyhoe speculates that Lieutenant Arnold encountered a remote-control observer unit controlled by extraterrestrials.

The Air Force offered a swift and predictable, if geographically puzzling, explanation. A short summary dated December 5 recounts Arnold's sighting but places him at San Antonio's Lackland Air Force Base instead of Laredo. The three-paragraph entry states in conclusion, "Probably a balloon."

Finally, an air intelligence report dated December 15 noted that the United States Department of Commerce Weather Bureau launched a lighted weather balloon in Laredo at 20:53 hours on December 4, about the time Lieutenant Arnold encountered his UFO. It adds, however, "Weather observers did not observe aircraft in the vicinity of the balloon. Neither tower nor any other aircraft observed light."

Gulf of Mexico, December 6

Two nights later, the crew of a B-29 bomber crossing the Gulf toward Galveston picked up some odd radar readings and saw amazing flashes of light.

Beyond that, the details get very sketchy.

Keyhoe once again chose to change the names of those involved, but in this case, he did not bother divulging that detail to readers. As a result, unknowing UFOlogists continue to perpetuate the story as fact, attributing the sightings to servicemen whose names could never be traced by today's historians. In Keyhoe's 1953 book, he dramatized dialogue between officers on the B-29 and added characters not mentioned in other reports.

The Gulf Coast area became a hot spot of UFO sightings that fall, especially around the port city of Mobile, Alabama. Ruppelt closely investigated a cluster of reports in September there at Brookley Air Force Base. They involved multiple visual and radar sightings, the sources of which remain unidentified. The Project Blue Book team also stood on heightened alert during this period because of the planned testing of the first hydrogen bomb. That explosion turned Elugelab Island of the Marshall Island chain into an underwater crater on November 1, 1952.

Surviving accounts of the story agree that the servicemen returned to a base somewhere near Galveston on December 6, after a night-training mission to Florida. Neither Keyhoe's book nor the available fragments of Project Blue Book indicate precisely which base the crew called home. The military had turned Galveston Army Airfield back over to local authorities for use as a municipal airport in November 1945. Perhaps the plane was normally hangared at Houston's Ellington Air Force Base, where navigators trained in 1952.

According to Project Blue Book excerpts, First Lieutenant Norman Karas was the first to notice something strange. He turned on his radar set around 5:30 a.m. and found unidentified blips moving toward the bomber at unbelievable speed. He timed them with a stopwatch, and a flight engineer instructor calculated the speed at 5,240 miles per hour. Karas recalibrated the radar set, but a second check brought the same results. He reported seeing about twenty targets all told, some of them coming within twenty miles of the plane.

"To the best of my knowledge, I believe that this object was real and moved at an extremely high speed and was not a malfunction or optical illusion," he is quoted in Project Blue Book as saying.

First Lieutenant William W. Naumann is also quoted in official accounts as saying the crew last saw the blips at 5:35 a.m. after radar signals "merged into a ½ inch curved arc about thirty miles from our aircraft at 320 degrees and proceeded across the scope and off it at a computed speed of over 9,000 miles per hour."

To Keyhoe's way of thinking, the blue-white flashes of light the crew witnessed were flying saucers traveling at colossal speeds. And what could the arc into which the radar blips merged be other than an alien mother ship?

A third interpretation of the Gulf of Mexico sighting comes from the Condon report.

According to the Condon group's analysis, a full moon lighted the B-29's 20,000-foot flight that night. When Karas turned on his radar set that clear, dry night, the crew should have been able to see refinery flares along the Louisiana coast with the naked eye. That the radarscope did not detect the nearby coastline should have been the crew's first clue that something was technologically amiss.

Condon surmised that an ever-popular temperature inversion caused the plane's own radar signals to bounce around and echo back to it, giving the impression of fast moving targets. The streaking lights, the report suggested, might have been Geminid meteors.

Despite Condon's after-the-fact analysis, a brief Project Blue Book entry classifies the Gulf of Mexico object as unidentified.

Whatever created unusual lights and radar blips over the Gulf that December may have come close enough to the coast for a few landlubbers to get a peek. The Houston *Post* and the Galveston *Daily News* both printed short articles after receiving numerous calls from readers that week. The papers reported similarly unusual lights seen at dusk on consecutive nights, but they gave different explanations.

The *Post*, apparently making little effort to investigate sightings on December 4, said the "silvery light, with a long trail stretching behind it" appeared to be a meteorite. The *Daily News* went to the trouble of making a few phone calls and was told by the CAA that lights seen between 5:30 and 6 p.m. on December 5 were rays of sunlight glinting off ice crystals along the vapor trails of two B-26 bombers from Fort Worth's Carswell Air Force Base. The planes had made a practice bombing run with Houston as a hypothetical target.

Like so many other things seen and, perhaps, willfully forgotten during the Cold War, the Gulf sighting may never be explained to the full satisfaction of those skeptical of the government's actions and motives. But if overt actions are any indication, even the military was not sure what to make of strange lights in the sky during the early 1950s.

A year after the Texas airmen encountered their UFOs, the Air Force announced it was setting up "flying saucer cameras" to help figure out whether would-be terrestrial or extraterrestrial invaders might be up to something. It also issued a fact sheet stating "the majority of all reported sightings have been found to involve either man-made objects such as aircraft or balloons, or known phenomena such as meteors and planets."

But just to be safe, the Air Force placed one of those flying saucer cameras right next door to Texas at Tinker Air Force Base in Oklahoma City.

Chapter 9:
Keeping Secrets:
A 1950s Pastime

At 8:30 p.m. on July 17, 1957, tens of thousands of Texans sat in their living rooms tuned in to one of the nation's most popular primetime television shows, "I've Got a Secret."

Hosted by crew-cut, bow-tie-wearing Garry Moore, an entertainer who got his start in radio, the thirty-minute CBS game show featured celebrity panelists Bill Cullen, Henry Morgan, Faye Emerson, and Jayne Meadows asking questions aimed at exposing the guest's often-silly secret. As the guest whispered his secret to Moore, the home audience read it on their screens, which made the probing by the witty Cullen, Morgan, Emerson, and Meadows and the guest's answers all the funnier.

Sponsored by Winston cigarettes (cartons of which Moore often gave guests), the live, black-and-white show usually featured two average Joe's or Jane's and one celebrity guest. On this summer night, veteran actor Don Ameche was the big name who tried to stump the panelists with his secret. Introduced from the studio audience was a young Marine aviator from Ohio, Major John Glenn, who the day before had set a new transcontinental speed record by flying a Dallas-built Chance-Vault F8U-1 Crusader fighter jet from California to New York in three hours, twenty-three minutes, and 8.4

seconds. Five years later, as one of the original Mercury 7 astronauts, he would be the first American to orbit the earth.

While cast members at CBS' studio in New York tried to ferret out the secrets of the show's guests that night, West Coast television and movie newsreel crews in Long Beach took in all the pageantry and cheesecake as forty-eight beauties vied to be crowned Miss USA for 1957.

One of the contestants, a green-eyed, long-legged brunette named Mary Leona Gage, grew up in the Piney Woods of East Texas, though on this night she represented the state of Maryland. She had borrowed forty-five dollars from her cousin to buy the gown she wore.

Like the guests getting grilled by the "I've Got a Secret" panelists, Miss Gage had her own secret: Though she claimed to be single and twenty-one years old, she was married, had two children, and was only eighteen, having married an airman stationed at Shepherd Air Force Base in Wichita Falls when she was fourteen and pregnant. Being married with children was nothing unusual during the post-World War II baby boom, but if the beauty contest judges found out Miss Maryland was actually Mrs. Maryland, she would be kicked out of the pageant. The rules said only single women could enter the competition, which gave young women a shot at a $2,000 prize, her very own trailer, and the prospect of commercial gain in product endorsements.

Later that night, after most Texans had gone to bed, Gage was crowned as Miss USA, her secret still intact.

Secrets in the Sky

But the U.S. Air Force was keeping an even bigger secret that night. Unknown but to a handful of people, earlier that day something had happened in the skies over Texas that the federal government would hold as top secret for more than a decade: An unidentified object trailed an RB-47H Air Force reconnaissance plane on a classified training mission for some

600 miles. UFO researchers still consider the incident, which lasted for more than an hour, one of the most mysterious UFO cases in the world.

The flight of Lacy 17 began routinely enough as Major Lewis D. Chase pushed the throttle forward to feed more fuel to the swept-wing plane's six General Electric turbojets as the specially outfitted Boeing "Stratojet" rolled down the runway at Forbes Air Force Base outside Topeka, Kansas, and soared into the night sky. As soon as Chase leveled out the aircraft, he assumed a course plotted by his navigator that would take the jet out over the Gulf of Mexico for a series of exercises covering gunnery, navigation, and the primary mission of the aircraft—electronic intelligence, which the Air Force called ELNIT.

All of this training would bring Chase and his crew up to speed for deployment to Germany, where the United States and its allies stood nose-to-nose against Communist East Germany, part of the Soviet empire. On board were co-pilot Captain James H. McCoid, navigator Captain Thomas H. Handley, and three electronic warfare officers: Captain Frank B. McClure, Captain Walter A. Tuchschner, and a noncommissioned officer, John J. Provenzano.

McClure, Tuchschner, and Provenzano belonged to the ranks of what the Air Force calls "Crows" because they used secret equipment to participate in black-operations missions. After takeoff on July 17, the trio crawled from their seats through a narrow, unpressurized passageway to a pressurized compartment in the bomb bay. This had to happen before the plane reached 10,000 feet.

Unlike radar, the sophisticated electronic equipment on board did not transmit signals. The blips that appeared on three monitors represented the origination points of electromagnetic signals emitted by other objects. Each picked up signals in a specific frequency range and analyzed their characteristics, including pulse.

By 4 a.m., the crew had completed their gunnery and navigation exercises over the Gulf of Mexico and had just flown back over land near Gulfport, Mississippi, when Captain McClure picked up a strong signal coming at the plane from behind its right beam, roughly at the 5 o'clock position. The signal was being transmitted at 2,995 to 3,000 megacycles, which McClure recognized as the frequency of S-band search radar. In other words, something was pinging the aircraft.

The captain knew that kind of signal came from ground-based radar, but this one seemed to emanate from something aloft in the predawn darkness over the Gulf. McClure concluded his scope must have gotten out of alignment. The signal had to be coming from a radar facility in Louisiana, he reasoned, not the open gulf.

While McClure endeavored to adjust his instrument, the signal's imprint moved up one side of his scope and then down the other. Unless his instrument had gone completely haywire, that meant whatever was transmitting the radar beam had just circled the plane. Then the strange signal went away, and McClure dismissed it as some anomaly. He said nothing about it over the jet's intercom system.

Up in the plastic-bubble cockpit, Major Chase flew westward over Jackson, Mississippi, on a course that would bring the jet over Texas. Soon the crew would begin the final segment of its training mission, a series of simulated electronic intelligence operations in concert with ground-based Air Force radar installations.

At 4:10 a.m. over Winnsboro, Louisiana, an intense white light with a bluish tint suddenly appeared in the pilot's field of vision at about 11 o'clock. Appearing to match the jet's altitude, the light closed rapidly on the aircraft. Thinking he must be seeing another aircraft's landing light, Chase shouted into his microphone for the crew to prepare for an evasive maneuver. Just as the pilot readied to execute a hard turn, the light changed direction and crossed the jet's flight path from left to right at seemingly incredible speed. The major and his co-pilot, who sat behind him, both saw the unidentified, fast-moving light. It had gone from an 11 o'clock to 2:30 o'clock position and then disappeared.

Chase informed the others on board what he and McCoid had just seen. Realizing now that his scope reading might not have been due to some equipment glitch, McClure reported the signal he had picked up.

Sitting with his two colleagues in the cramped, windowless ELNIT compartment in the belly of the plane, McClure readjusted his scope at 4:30 a.m. to detect signals in the same frequency range he had picked up earlier. Provenzano also adjusted his scope to a setting that would receive a signal in the 3,000-megahertz range. Almost immediately McClure found a strong signal reaching the aircraft from roughly the same direction the light had moved toward. Provenzano's monitor also picked up the signal. The transmissions appeared to be coming from the same location, the source keeping pace with the plane, which was flying at more than 500 miles an hour.

At this point, the military aircraft soared over East Texas at 34,000 feet heading toward the Dallas-Fort Worth area. The sky was clear. Staying in constant contact with McClure, the pilot increased the jet's speed. The two scope operators monitoring the mystery signal reported that it kept up with the plane, maintaining the same bearing.

Nine minutes after two of the aircraft's monitors had acquired the signal (the third, manned by Captain Tuchschner, was designed to receive only lower frequencies and played no role in the incident), Major Chase saw a large light he estimated as about 5,000 feet below and to the right of the converted bomber at about 2 o'clock. The pilot could not make out the shape or size of the object, but the light appeared to be coming from the top of whatever it was.

One minute later, at 4:40 a.m., McClure said he picked up signals from two locations, one at forty degrees bearing and one at seventy degrees. The pilot and co-pilot confirmed they now saw red lights at both points.

Chase contacted an Air Force radar installation at Duncanville that was to have been involved in that night's exercise and requested permission to divert from the flight plan and pursue the unidentified contacts. He also requested, as the Air Force later reported, "all assistance possible." The major got the clearance he requested, both from the Duncanville Air Force facility and civilian air traffic controllers in the tower at Dallas' Love Field.

Then the Duncanville radar operators asked for the coordinates of the mystery signals and confirmed that they were tracking the same objects. Whatever was shadowing Chase's aircraft, it had now been seen by the pilot and his co-pilot, detected by two of the aircraft's instruments, and picked up by the closest ground radar.

Chase increased his airspeed and turned to pursue the object, but it stopped and the jet over flew it. At 4:52 a.m., the light and signals disappeared.

By now the plane had crossed the Dallas-Fort Worth area and continued west over Mineral Wells. Chase pulled the aircraft to the left and the light reappeared, visually and on McClure's instrument as well as the ground radar. This time, it appeared as a single signal.

Now the object looked to be about five miles away. Chase brought the jet back around on a course toward the object, which dropped to 15,000 feet and disappeared again.

Three minutes later, at 4:55 a.m., the pilot radioed that he needed to resume his flight plan because the plane was running low on fuel. The radio operator in Duncanville replied affirmatively when asked whether he had reported the night's events through official military channels.

At 4:57 a.m., McClure reacquired the mystery signal, and a minute later Chase saw the light again. The RB-47H was now about twenty nautical miles northwest of Fort Worth with the light at about 20,000 feet at 2'oclock. The object appeared to follow the jet almost all the way to Oklahoma City before disappearing for good.

When Chase landed at Forbes AFB in Topeka, he faced more than a routine post-flight debriefing. The intelligence officer for the Strategic Air Command's 55th Reconnaissance Wing interviewed the six crewmembers at length, later forwarding a four-page summary report to headquarters at Ent Air Force Base in Colorado. In November, the summary and a twelve-page report on the incident written by Major Chase on September 10 were sent to the Air Force's Project Bluebook office at Wright-Patterson Air Force Base in Dayton, Ohio.

A Close Call

An unknown object had stalked a military aircraft and had been detected by the plane's six-man crew and ground radar, but the public remained ignorant of the unusual event. However, newspapers did report another aircraft's unusual experience over Texas about half an hour before the RB-47H encounter began.

The El Paso *Herald-Post*, an evening newspaper, published a page-one story on July 18 about a near collision midair east of El Paso involving an American Airlines DC-6 with eighty-five people aboard.

American Flight 655, piloted by Captain Ed Bachner, had been enroute from Dallas to Los Angeles at 3:29 a.m. on July 17 when Bachner spotted what appeared to be a large set of lights on a collision course with his aircraft. The Fort Worth-based captain pushed his plane's nose down for a steep dive to avoid crashing into the other object.

Bachner radioed the El Paso tower to report the incident and said he would land to drop off two passengers injured when thrown from their seats by the sudden emergency maneuver.

Bachner flew under visual flight rules that clear night. The incident happened over an area known as the Salt Flat about sixty miles east of El Paso, apparently outside any radar coverage.

Though Bachner said he dove to avoid an aircraft "at least as large as an Air Force B-47 bomber," El Paso's Biggs Air Force Base reported no aircraft aloft at the time. And no civilian pilot came forth to reveal a role in the incident despite Bachner's estimate that his plane missed the other craft by only fifty feet.

"We and the military are making every effort to find out who was flying in the area at the time," a spokesman for the Civil Aeronautics Administration told the border city newspaper.

One of the crew members aboard American 655 that night was Argie Hoskins, a young woman from El Paso who had just completed her training as a flight attendant (then called stewardesses) that spring.

"One evening flying between El Paso and Douglas [Arizona]," she later recalled on an internet blog, "the pilot lower[ed] the plane very quickly. He reported that he had picked up an unidentified object in our path. He was not asleep at the wheel. Speaking of such! I flew with a flight engineer that shared that he believed in UFOs because of the things that he had observed while flying."

The retired flight attendant had the location slightly wrong—the incident happened before the plane reached El Paso—but nearly a half-century later she still remembered it clearly.

RB-47 Project Blue Book card

The next day's El Paso newspapers printed no follow-up coverage. In fact, the public learned nothing more of the incident until August 2, when the *Herald-Post* ran a story that the "mystery ship" in the July 17 near miss had been another commercial airliner. The story, which came from the newspaper's Washington bureau and cited "sources on the Hill," did not identify the other airline involved. A flight timetable from that era found online shows National Airlines

Flight 966 to be headed toward Dallas-Fort Worth at about the time of the incident.

A year earlier, 128 people died when two commercial airliners crashed over the Grand Canyon. That accident should have heightened concern over air safety, but the Texas incident received remarkably little public exposure. Bizarrely, a Project Blue Book card file on the RB-47H incident noted that the mystery light seen by Major Chase and his co-pilot on the night of July 18, 1957, had been identified as American Airlines Flight 655, an obvious impossibility.

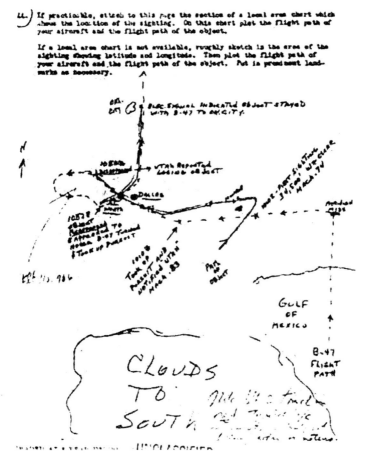

Records Opened, but Mystery Remains

No one outside the military knew about the so-called RB-47 incident until 1968, when researchers working on the University of Colorado's Condon Report discovered the eleven-year-old case. The study they published in 1969 devoted 2,260 words to the incident, though its authors admitted they failed to locate any military records concerning it. While they interviewed three of the Lacy 17 crewmembers, the investigators could not come up with an explanation for the incident. "The phenomenon remains unidentified," they concluded.

Physicist James E. McDonald did the most detailed digging into the RB-47 case in the late 1960s and early 1970s prior to his suicide at the age of 51 on June 13, 1971, near Tucson, Arizona. The Condon researchers could not find any Air Force records pertaining to the case because they researched the wrong date, he discovered. After determining the correct date, McDonald obtained all the military records concerning the case through Federal Freedom of Information Act (FOIA) requests. He also interviewed all of the crewmembers. McDonald presented his findings in papers delivered to the American Association for the Advancement of Science in 1969 and to the American Institute for Aeronautics and Astronautics in 1971.

But McDonald did not get the last word on the RB-47 case. UFO researchers continued to debate the incident, with skeptics attempting to debunk it as the product of instrument malfunction and true believers countering with their own interpretations of the available information.

Just what played cat-and-mouse with the crew of the most sophisticated American aircraft of its day in the skies over Texas that July 17, 1957, remains a mystery.

The final resolution of one of the other secrets being kept that night is more easily explained. The day after her selection as Miss USA, Mary Leona Gage tearfully admitted her deception and forfeited her tiara.

CHAPTER 10:
LEVELLAND'S "FIERY OBJECT" STOPPED CARS

South Plains readers of the November 3, 1957, Lubbock *Avalanche-Journal* woke up to two startling pieces of news that Sunday morning.

The Russians had launched a second satellite, this time with a dog named Laika aboard. Now, the Soviet Union could claim not only the world's first orbiting device, a radio transmitting object called Sputnik that had been launched on October 4 that year, but the first living thing sent into space from Earth.

While the American public found news of the Soviet Union's technological advances worrisome in light of increasing Cold War tensions, another headline that day raised fears that the United States might be facing a threat greater than communism: "Near Levelland—Flying 'Fiery Object' Seen." The story started off with only three words, "What was it?"

Shortly before 11 p.m. on November 2, dispatcher A.J. Fowler answered the phone in the radio room of the Levelland Police Department. The call came from farm worker Pedro Saucedo, a thirty-year-old Korean War veteran. He told Fowler that he and a friend, Joe Salaz, had been driving along State Highway 114 four miles west of the Hockley County cotton and oil town of 10,000 when something extremely bright appeared in the sky over his truck.

Saucedo said his truck's engine died and the headlights went out when the object flew over it. The truck driver and his friend got out of the stalled vehicle and felt so much heat they "hit the ground," as he later put it.

"It...had colors—yellow, white—and it looked like a torpedo, about 200 feet long, moving about 600 to 800 miles an hour," Saucedo said.

Once the object had passed, the man continued, his vehicle's headlights flashed back on. Climbing back behind the wheel of his truck, he turned his key in the ignition and the engine started with no problem. Since the aerial object appeared to be headed east toward Levelland, Saucedo and his friend sped in the opposite direction to Whiteface, a small Cochran County community about fourteen miles from Levelland. There they stopped and used a pay phone to call the police.

Saucedo's excited report did not impress the law enforcement dispatcher, who dismissed it as a crank call possibly inspired by imbibing too much beer on a Saturday night. He logged it but took no other action.

Just before midnight another call came through from someone reporting a similar unusual occurrence. A man who identified himself as Jim Wheeler told Fowler that he had been four miles east of town on Highway 114 (misidentified as Highway 116 in most accounts) when he saw a bright, egg-shaped object that looked to be 200 feet wide resting on the pavement. As he neared the thing, the man related, his car died.

When Wheeler emerged from his vehicle, the object rose into the night sky, went dark, and disappeared. Getting back in his car, he found that the engine turned over with no difficulty.

Shortly after Wheeler's call, the Levelland dispatcher logged a call from Jose Alvarez, who was in Whitharral, eleven miles north of town. He, too, had seen a strange light that killed his car engine for a time

Finally grasping that something unusual must be going on, Fowler alerted the handful of officers on patrol that night of the reports that had been coming in. He also notified Sheriff Weir Clem. Thirty-two miles east of Levelland, authorities in Lubbock monitored that radio traffic, and in turn, a reporter for the *Avalanche-Journal* heard about it. The reporter called the Levelland Police Department to ask what was going on.

Dispatcher Fowler told the journalist that his telephone had been ringing off the hook. "They are driving us crazy," he said. All the callers seemed upset by what they said they had seen, and some sounded terrified, the officer said.

Not everyone who saw the mysterious object reported it immediately. Newell Wright, Jr., a nineteen-year-old student at Lubbock's Texas Technological College, was on his way home from Lubbock at 12:05 a.m. when his car stalled out about nine miles east of Levelland. He pushed in the clutch and shifted to neutral, letting the vehicle coast to the shoulder of the road. Then he got out and raised the hood to look for what he supposed to be a battery problem. Not finding anything out of order, he slammed the hood down and wondered what to do next. That's when he noticed a bluish-green object farther down the highway. As he looked at it, the object rose and soon vanished. When he tried to start his car, it worked like normal. "I then proceeded home very slowly," he later said.

Though the article on the Levelland sightings that ran in the Sunday edition of the Lubbock newspaper included only twelve paragraphs and had been hurriedly thrown together in the wee hours of the morning, the Associated Press rewrote the story and distributed it to all its clients. That focused worldwide attention on the small Texas town. The *Avalanche-Journal* followed up with a much more detailed report on Monday morning, November 4.

"Levelland 'Flaming Thing' Brings World Knocking At City's Door," the Lubbock newspaper said in a five-column headline at the bottom of page one. Reporter Bill Wilkerson had found seven people who said they had seen the "thing" up close, with even more claiming they had seen it from a distance.

"The object was described by most observers as being a 200-foot long, egg-shaped ball of fire that moved at a great speed," the article summarized. "It was reportedly sighted during a two-and-a-half hour period at points four to ten miles from Levelland to the east, north and west."

After the first several calls came in that night, Fowler related, he called the Lubbock Police Department and Reese Air Force Base on Lubbock's west side. A duty officer at Reese said none of the base's aircraft had been flying at the time. Similarly, the Civil Aeronautics Administration's (predecessor of the Federal Aviation Administration) Lubbock operation said it had not been tracking any planes in the Levelland area at the time of the mass sighting of the mystery object.

Sheriff Clem, a year into his third two-year term, had been home when the first call came in that night, but when Fowler informed him that he was getting more and more reports from worried citizens, the sheriff strapped on his pistol and joined other officers in the field.

Not long after the sheriff and deputy Pat McCullough hit the road, a fiery object streaked across the highway in front of the county lawman's vehicle as he drove south toward Levelland on what local residents called the Oklahoma Flat Road. Several miles behind the sheriff, two state troopers stationed at nearby Littlefield, Floyd Gavin and Lee Hargrove, also saw what looked like a flash of fire.

Trooper Hargrove later said in a signed statement:

> Was driving south on the unmarked roadway known as Oklahoma Flat Highway and was attempting to search for an unidentified object reported by the Levelland Police Department.... I saw a strange-looking flash, which looked to be down the roadway approximately a mile to a mile and a half.... The flash went from east to west and appeared to be close to the ground.

Unlike some of the civilian witnesses, the law enforcement officers did not experience any difficulties with their vehicles when they saw whatever it was. But Ray Jones, Levelland's fire marshal, later said his vehicle's headlights had dimmed and the engine hesitated momentarily when he saw the mystery light.

Fowler had received fifteen telephone calls that Saturday night and early Sunday morning from people who said they had seen something in the sky around Levelland. Of those, seven witnesses reported vehicle problems associated with the object.

At midmorning Sunday, with no additional sightings having been reported, most of the officers called it a night. But Sheriff Clem did not get much sleep. Once word of the Levelland sightings hit the news wires, phones in his office and at the Levelland Police Department lit up like the lights on a drilling rig.

"All I've done all day is answer my telephone," Clem told the Lubbock newspaper. "People have called from New York, Los Angeles and it seems like every other town in the country." In so many words, each caller got essentially the same comment the sheriff made to the *Avalanche-Journal*: "I definitely know there was something. I know it from not having any controversy between those who saw it. Their stories fit to a T."

Later that morning, authorities contacted Saucedo and asked him to come to the Levelland police station to provide a more detailed account of what he had seen the night before. Officer Shelby Hall typed up what Saucedo had to say and had him sign it. The witness also talked with the reporter from the Lubbock newspaper.

"I was driving out to the Gerald Redding [the statement misspelled his last name with one "d"] farm near Pettit…with a friend, Joe Salaz, when we first saw the thing," Saucedo said. "We first saw a flash of light in a field to our right and we didn't think much about it at first."

Saucedo's statement continued:

> Then it rose up out of the field and started toward us, picking up speed. When it got near, the lights of my truck went out and the motor died. I jumped out of the truck and hit the deck because I was afraid.
>
> I called to Joe but he didn't get out. The thing passed directly over my truck with a great sound and rush of wind. It sounded like thunder and my truck rocked from the blast. I felt a lot of heat.
>
> Then I got up and watched it go out of sight toward Levelland. We drove on to Whiteface to call police and we stopped at a feed mill where a man told us that

someone else had just told him about it.

While reporter Wilkerson gathered information for his Monday morning story, two more people came forward to report having seen the object the night before.

Wright, his parents out of town for the weekend, had driven straight home after seeing the light earlier that Sunday morning. He had not told anyone about what he had seen for fear of ridicule, but after talking to his folks, he decided to report the incident to the sheriff. He called at 1:30 p.m. that day and agreed to give a written statement.

Ronald Martin, an eighteen-year-old truck driver, said his truck died and the lights went out about 12:45 a.m. that day when "a big ball of fire dropped on the highway" in front of his vehicle on Highway 114 about five miles west of Levelland. That location was only about a mile from where Saucedo had first seen the object.

Changing colors to a bluish-green, the object alighted on the two-lane highway as Martin watched.

"I guess I sat there in the truck about fifteen minutes, too astounded to move, then it took off," Martin said.

When the object became airborne again, he continued, it changed back into a fireball and went straight up into the sky before disappearing.

Though something described as a fireball on asphalt pavement should have left scorch marks, officers checking the areas of the reported sightings found nothing unusual on the highway or adjacent right of way. Reese Air Base also sent personnel to investigate, but reported they did not find anything out of the ordinary. (Interviewed years later, one of Sheriff Clem's daughters said that not long after the sightings her father had received a call from a rancher northeast of Levelland to come take a look at something unusual: a ring-shaped burned spot on the ground. Another woman, a girl in 1957, said her father had shown her the mysterious burned area that weekend. Possibly considering it a hoax, Clem never mentioned the burned grass publicly.)

Earlier that Sunday, a fifty-seven-year-old Abilene medical supply firm owner, James A. Lee, read about the Levelland sightings in his hometown daily with more than casual interest. An amateur radio operator and director of a UFO study group he called the Interplanetary Space Patrol, Lee had been scheduled to speak to a HAM radio club in Brownfield that afternoon. His subject was UFOs. Lee drove to Brownfield, gave his talk and then drove the twenty-nine miles from there to Littlefield. Using a bulky portable tape recorder, he spent the rest of the evening interviewing some of the people who had seen the lights the night before.

That evening, the Levelland story made national television. Correspondent Robert Pierpoint, reporting from Washington for CBS News, said:

> Folks in Levelland, Texas are worried about strange objects in their neighborhood. Sheriff Weir Clem says he has received several reports of a strange, egg-shaped object, about 200 feet long, landing on farms and highways last night in the vicinity of Levelland. Sheriff Clem said he even got a glimpse of this thing, which somehow switched off lights and auto engines when it came near. The sheriff said lights and engines worked fine again after the thing went away.

Federal Interest

On Monday, the Air Force said it would begin an investigation into the Levelland sightings. The day before, in fact, a captain working as acting counterintelligence officer at Reese AFB had sent a teletype summarizing the Levelland reports to the Air Force's Office of Special Investigations. The

"TWX," as those landline messages were called at the time, concluded: "No idea of the possible cause of the sighting."

Also on November 4, Bill Haggard, public information officer for the White Sands, New Mexico, Proving Grounds—345 miles from Lubbock—disclosed an unusual report made by two military policemen at the sprawling top-secret government reservation. Both MPs said they had seen a ball of fire in the sky over the proving grounds about 3 a.m. the day before. The men said the object looked to be about 200 feet long and 75 feet wide. The MPs said the thing they saw appeared to be hovering above the no-longer-used bunkers that once sheltered scientists and technicians who observed the first atomic bomb explosion on July 16, 1945. After remaining motionless in the air for a time, the object moved off at a forty-five-degree angle. The light began to pulse on and off before it disappeared.

News reports of the sightings in West Texas moved U.S. Representative J.T. Rutherford of Odessa to write the Pentagon demanding an explanation for whatever had happened around Levelland, which lay in his district. Unknown to the congressman, an Air Force UFO investigator from the Air Defense Command headquarters at Colorado Springs, Colorado had arrived in Lubbock on November 4. Staff Sergeant Norman P. Barth had taken a commercial flight to Lubbock and stayed until November 6 gathering details for his report. The Lubbock air base would not give the investigator's name to the news media, and he did not do any interviews.

"If this thing is American," the West Texas Congressman told the Lubbock newspaper, "there should be some explanation—at least to the people of the area—that it is an American experiment so they will not be alarmed."

Well aware that many of his rural constituents kept rifles or shotguns in their pickup trucks and homes, the Congressman worried that someone—or some thing— might get hurt.

"We certainly don't want anybody to harm such an object or its occupants if it's American," he continued. "But if it's not

American, the people should be notified so they can do something, like declare open season on it."

Another Congressman, Representative Walter Rogers of Pampa, offered more practical advice in his next newsletter to constituents: Don't be too quick to report flying saucers. Rogers wrote that someone had told him that a man from Nebraska who had reported seeing the landing of an alien spacecraft and talking with its crew had been committed to a mental institution. Particularly vulnerable to a trip to the funny farm were those who told and retold their stories, the congressman continued.

"According to the new rules," Rogers wrote without explaining whose rules they were, "if you tell the story the same way every time, you are possessed of a fixation...and therefore subject to being confined in the mental institution."

The smartest tactic for anyone seeing a UFO, the Pampa lawmaker went on, was not to repeat the story "until you find out what rule is being applied in [your] locality." Rogers' bottom line: "It might be best to say nothing."

While some of the Panhandle congressman's constituents may have taken his advice and kept their mouths shut after having seen a UFO, many people in Texas, the United States, and the world felt no such constraint that year. Indeed, 1957 marked the third of the Cold War era's major waves of UFO sighting, the other years being 1947 and 1952.

One of those not afraid to speak out about UFOs was the head of the Interplanetary Space Patrol, the businessman from Abilene. Two days after visiting Levelland and tape recording some of the people who had seen the lights, Lee pronounced that they were definitely intelligently controlled.

"Whatever this thing was it had a definite mission and a plan in operation," Lee told a reporter for the Dallas *Morning News*. Calling it an "amazing, fantastic story," he continued: "Those people out there saw something—there's no question about it. It was literally something out of this world."

Lee believed sightings of UFOs often occurred just prior to public events at which UFOs were to be discussed, such as his previously scheduled talk in Brownfield. "It's a matter of conditioning the minds of the people" for a mass arrival on Earth, he continued. "They will soon come in large numbers for all to see, and the skeptics will not have a leg left to stand on."

The alien invasion never came, and Lee refocused his efforts to organize satellite-watching programs after the United States launched its first manmade moon (another word for satellites) in 1958.

The publicity generated by all the sightings clearly inspired hoaxers, as well. Three days after the Levelland sightings, the Dallas County Sheriff's Office got inundated with telephone calls that a "flying saucer" had landed near Grapevine in Tarrant County. Calls from the public also lit up law enforcement switchboards in nearby Fort Worth.

A couple in Grapevine reported seeing a glowing, transparent balloon-shaped object west of Royal Lane on State Highway 114, the same highway that passes through Levelland, 334 miles to the northwest. Officers went to the scene but did not find anything unusual. Following additional investigation, the next day Grapevine Police Chief John Baze said the reported UFO sighting had turned out to be a hoax on the part of five persons.

Less than two weeks after the Levelland sightings, Congressman Rutherford got his answer from the military. The Air Force on November 15 distributed a news release dealing with the Levelland incident and other recent reported sightings. The portion on Levelland read:

> Levelland, Texas: (Big light, seen by 'dozens,' stalled autos.) Investigation on the scene revealed that only three persons,

rather than 'dozens,' could be located who saw the 'big light.' Preliminary reports have not revealed cause of 'stalled' automobiles at this time, although rain and electrical storms at the time of the reported sightings, affecting wet electrical circuits, could be cause. Object visible only few seconds, not sustained visibility as had been implied.

Evaluation: Weather phenomenon of electrical nature, generally classified as 'ball lightning' or 'St. Elmo's Fire,' caused by stormy conditions in the area, including mist, rain, thunderstorms and lightning.

The Air Force report said no UFO evidence had been found and that all but two percent of all UFO cases reported had been explained. Though not publicly known for years, the Air Force investigator talked to only three witnesses in addition to Sheriff Clem, whose daughter later revealed had been told by the Air Force to "forget that he had ever seen anything."

Later Investigations

The Levelland community, meanwhile, took the incident in stride. While some believed they had seen something from another world, others agreed with the Air Force that it had been some sort of natural phenomenon and still others found humor in it. Someone, for instance, put an official-looking sign outside town that read: "Caution Flying Saucers Landing on Highways."

A decade later, Dr. James E. McDonald, senior physicist at the University of Arizona's Institute for Atmospheric Physics and a professor in that university's meteorology department, reviewed the Air Force's report on the Levelland sights. He debunked the theory that the mysterious lights were ball lighting. "I dug out the weather maps and rainfall data," he wrote in 1967. "A large, high-pressure area was moving southward over the Texas Panhandle, completely antithetical to convective activity and lightning of any sort."

SIGN OF THE TIMES—The City of Lubbock's traffic safety department, with tongue in cheeks, erected this sign on the Levelland highway in western Lubbock Wednesday. Miss Martha Kenley, 19, a Texas Tech coed from San Angelo, pays no attention to the sign but—like just about everyone else—was anxious to talk about the cigar-shaped unidentified object sighted near Levelland by several persons several days ago. (Staff Photo by Kenneth May.)

When the Air Force contracted with the University of Colorado to do an extensive scientific investigation of the UFO phenomena, a team of researchers directed by Dr. Edward Condon looked at vehicle interference cases in general, but the scientists did not specifically investigate the Levelland incident. The Condon Committee's 1968 report ran to 1,485 pages but included only one mention of Levelland in a section titled "Automobile Engine Malfunction and Headlight Failure." The authors noted: "Magnetic mapping of the bodies of automobiles involved in particularly puzzling UFO reports of past years, such as the November 1957 incidents at Levelland, Texas, would have been most desirable, but the cars were no longer available for study."

In his 1972 book *The UFO Experience: A Scientific Inquiry*, J. Allen Hynek, who in 1957 had been scientific advisor for Project Blue Book, said the Air Force should have taken the Levelland incident more seriously. He wrote:

> Caption Gregory, then head of Blue Book, did call me... [concerning Levelland], but at that time, as the person directly responsible for the tracking of the new Russian satellite, I was on a virtual around-the-clock duty and... unable to give it any attention whatever. I am not proud today that I hastily concurred in Captain Gregory's evaluation as 'ball lightning' on the basis of information that an electrical storm had been in progress in the Levelland area at the time. That was shown not to be the case....Besides, had I

given it any thought whatever, I would soon have recognized the absence of any evidence that ball lightning can stop cars and put out headlights.

Some twenty-five years later, researcher Antonio F. Rullan undertook a study of the 1957 sightings. He cataloged 209 reported UFO cases in the Southwest—more than half of them in Texas—during the final quarter of 1957. New Mexico had the second-most sightings, nearly 25 percent of the cases.

The first Texas sighting during the peak month of November 1957 came at 2 a.m. on the first day of the month, when someone near Coleman witnessed an oblong, reddish object alternately hovering above and maneuvering near an oil rig. At 6:20 a.m. that same day, a woman saw a glowing oblong object in the Sandia Mountains of New Mexico. On November 2, more than two hours prior to the first Levelland sighting, someone saw an unidentified object south of Amarillo. Whatever it was, it caused car engines to stall.

More significant than the numbers involved was that the 1957 wave brought the first significant reporting of what ufologists call vehicle interference (VI) cases. Of the Southwestern UFO reports, twenty-four involved VI and three-fourths of those were attributed to mysterious nighttime lights such as the "what's it" seen by so many people around Levelland.

The Levelland case and similar reported occurrences, Rullan wrote, likely are attributable to one of four factors: Social contagion (people figuratively saying "Me, too!" after an initial well-publicized sighting); ball lightning; unknown atmospheric phenomenon; or "intelligently controlled unknown object."

Rullan concluded: "Given the diverse descriptions of what was observed during this wave, the causes…very likely include the presence of real, unknown phenomenon (which triggered the start of the wave and continued its presence...) plus social contagion." The "unknown" could either have been natural or intelligently controlled, but "we cannot reject either hypothesis because of the poor data quality and weak evidence in most of the cases."

A final theory popular among some conspiracy theorists holds that the 1957 Levelland sightings had nothing to do with natural phenomena or visitors from another world. As Peter Brookesmith noted in his book *UFO: The Government Files*: "More than one ufologist has suggested that the Levelland flap was engineered by clandestine government agencies to distract attention from the Sputnik launch and the Soviet space program, which was then markedly more successful than the comparable US effort."

Still, after all these years, the question remains. What was it?

CHAPTER 11:
A TEXAS UFO FACTORY:
COLUMBIA SCIENTIFIC
BALLOON FACILITY

Official government sources and general debunkers often turn to the humble weather balloon to explain what the untrained eye might honestly mistake for a flying saucer. Texans inevitably spotted their share in decades past, what with the world's most advanced scientific balloon launching pad sitting right there in bucolic Palestine. Since the mid-1960s, scientists have been letting loose billowing plastic behemoths that make standard weather balloons look like decorations at a child's birthday party.

The Columbia Scientific Balloon Facility (CSBF) sends some of the largest balloons known to man to the edge of space. They float up twenty miles—higher than planes fly but lower than satellites—above 99.5 percent of Earth's atmosphere. They measure what is up there, gaze back down at us, and peer into the cosmos.

"It's like a cheap ride into space," said site manager Danny Ball.

A Generation of Scientists

The National Science Foundation (NSF) founded the facility in Boulder, Colorado, in 1961. Two years later, communities in Oklahoma, Arkansas, and Texas competed to become its permanent home. The NSF wanted a centrally located telemetry station with predictable wind patterns and no commercial flight paths overhead. A sparse population for two to three hundred miles around would decrease the risk of an experiment package parachuting onto someone's roof. Palestine, located south of Tyler, had all of that—and Texan Lyndon B. Johnson in the White House.

Then called the National Scientific Balloon Facility (NSBF), the site existed primarily to help future scientists get their PhDs, Ball explained. Physics and astronomy graduate students needed a place they could develop hypotheses, design experiments, fly them nearly to outer space, and analyze the data. In the 1960s and '70s, sixty to seventy balloons a year rose into the East Texas sky. They flew in every direction, sometimes landing three or four states away.

Over a couple of decades, the students' experiments answered most of the "simple" scientific questions about that fringe where Earth's atmosphere ends and space begins. The experiments became more sophisticated and needed to fly longer, so the balloons grew bigger and more expensive. Back in 1963, the average scientific balloon held 2.8 million cubic feet of helium. Today's most commonly flown balloons capture 40 million cubic feet.

Imagine the Astrodome inside a plastic bubble floating 120,000 feet in the air.

Gradually, the experiments became too grand to entrust to graduate students. Cost inflated from thousands of dollars into tens of millions. Still, scientists can test their theories much more cheaply, surely, and quickly with balloons than by hoping for a coveted slot on a rocket or the Space Shuttle. As a result of this trend toward more advanced science, the facility in 1982 transferred from the NSF to the National Aeronautics and Space Administration (NASA). New Mexico State University's Physical Science Laboratory now holds its operations contract and reports to the Goddard Space Flight Center's Wallops Flight Facility.

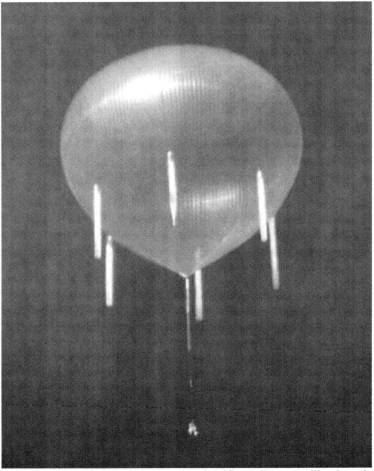

In the 1960s and '70s, the National Scientific Balloon Facility launched sixty to seventy balloons a year into the East Texas sky. Now renamed for the space shuttle and its crew that crashed in the area, the Columbia Scientific Balloon Facility today mostly prepares much larger and more sophisticated balloons for launch elsewhere. Pictured here is a 40-million-cubic-foot, zero-pressure model. (Photo courtesy of National Aeronautics and Space Administration, Columbia Scientific Balloon Facility.)

The CSBF's mission still includes an educational component, but full-fledged scientists design most of the experiments these days. They study cosmic rays, the magnetosphere, and distant stars. Sometimes, their work paves the way for experiments performed on spacecraft or in supercollider labs. A notable 1979 mission gave New Mexico State scientists important insights into antimatter.

More sophisticated, expensive payloads mean fewer flights. CSBF launches only about fifteen flights a year now, and only a couple of those take off from Palestine. Population growth in East Texas makes keeping unwanted deliveries out of people's backyards more difficult. The only balloons launched from Palestine now fly in the summer.

"All of them come down in West Texas, about three hundred miles from here around the Midland/Odessa area," Ball said.

Back in August 1998, a 2,200-pound telescope crashed into some power lines in an Andrews oil field. Scientists always run the risk of losing years of work when they place it at the mercy of air currents, but such unfortunate landings are by far the exception rather than the rule.

Balloons or Flying Saucers?

Most of CSBF's domestic balloon launches now occur at a World War II-era Army airfield in Fort Sumner, New Mexico. The small community, where the bones of Billy the Kid lie, sits about equidistant east of Clovis and north of Roswell. NSBF opened the remote facility in 1987 because East Texas just got too crowded.

"If we have one pass within a hundred miles of Albuquerque at sunset, we will have all kinds of calls," Ball said. "Our flights are routinely turned in as UFO reports. It happens all the time."

The giant, teardrop-shaped balloons consist of the same polyethylene film used to make plastic bags. They cost tens of thousands of dollars and only fly once. The balloons take off filled to only about to one twenty-fifth capacity; the helium expands as they rise and the atmosphere thins, Ball explained. A fully extended, unpacked parachute dangles underneath, with valuable scientific payload hanging below that. A balloon might carry aloft a package as small as a four-foot cube or as large as a forty-foot-tall telescope. A strobe light on top flashes only until the balloon gets above airplane altitude.

From twenty miles below, Earthlings cannot see the relatively tiny payloads. The balloons themselves look like jellyfish in the sky during the day. Things really get interesting just before dark.

"When the sun sets on them, they glow eerily for a while, turn orange, then blink off," Ball said. "If I didn't know what they are, I'd probably think it was a UFO, too."

If a witness calls the Federal Aviation Administration or a nearby Air Force base, the person who answers the phone usually knows about the CSBF and maybe even the particular launch responsible for the sighting. Less informed sheriff's deputies or news assignments editors may not know who to call to check out such things. They can leave witnesses, or entire communities, thinking something truly mysterious paid a visit.

Another opportunity for misidentification comes when payloads land. Airplanes accompany balloons as they ascend, then take back to the skies to bring the cargo down. The aircraft look for good landing spots, places clear of houses and large bodies of water. Flight commanders remotely signal balloons to separate from their parachutes, which float payloads back to the Earth. Descent takes about forty-five minutes. Ground teams then track and retrieve the experiments, sometimes battling the elements and wildlife. When a package lands at night, the team must wait until sunrise to look for it. This sets the occasional early rising farmer up for quite a shock.

"They get pretty excited. Some of these things look like spaceships from another planet or something," Ball said. Some witnesses' imaginations can get the best of them, too, like the group in Weatherford who reported a hot air balloon crashing with six people inside. "I think there was a little beer involved in that," Ball surmised.

Back in October 1987, while the Palestine facility still flew balloons more frequently and in more directions, one landing gave a pair of siblings near Bratt, Florida, a rude awakening. A ten-by-six-foot white box ended up in Sandra Slate's backyard.

"It just lit the whole place up out here," Slate told the St. Petersburg *Times*. "We were afraid to go out."

"It just sounded like trains coming through," added her brother, Danny Lowery. "I didn't know what was going on."

Texans encountered such surprises more frequently through the middle of the Cold War when students sent experiments aloft regularly. The facility's early administrators sought little attention, so most Texans did not even know that one of the world's top scientific balloon installations called Palestine home. No one could blame witnesses for being shocked to see one of its projects glowing at sunset or landing behind a barn.

NASA's public-relations machine did shine a light on the facility shortly after the agency took it over in the mid-1980s. Newspapers like the New York *Times* and the *Wall Street Journal* wrote lengthy features. But the number of flights in general—and from Palestine in particular—had already begun dropping off by then.

Unfortunately, CSBF does not have a comprehensive log of flights from the 1960s and 1970s. Ball emphasizes, however, that CSBF is all about pure science—it never sent up any classified missions for the Department of Defense.

Staff can look up flights from the 1980s forward, but Ball—an admitted UFO skeptic—could not solve any of the more recent mystery sightings recounted in this book.

A New Name

The NSBF became a hub of activity after the Space Shuttle Columbia disintegrated on re-entry into our atmosphere on February 1, 2003. The debris trailed from just north of Palestine to the Louisiana border. About three hundred people from NASA, the National Guard, the U.S. Forest Service, and the Texas Department of Public Safety used the balloon facility as a staging area for recovery efforts.

Later, local civic leaders approached U.S. Representative Jeb Hensarling of Dallas about honoring the Columbia's crew. Hensarling proposed changing the balloon facility's name, and NASA made it official three years after the crash.

"This tribute to the crew of the Space Shuttle Columbia is in recognition of the dedication and sacrifice made by those brave individuals willing to risk their lives to further humanity's knowledge about space exploration," Vernon Jones said in a press release. Jones is senior scientist for suborbital research at NASA's Science Mission Directorate, which manages the balloon facility.

CSBF continues to aid the space program and build general scientific knowledge about the Earth and the cosmos, even though fewer balloons fly from Palestine these days. The facility maintains a full-time staff of about eighty people, and visiting scientists from around the world spend weeks or months there preparing experiment packages before flights that launch from Antarctica or northern Sweden with increasing frequency. Scientists like these extreme locales because balloons can stay up longer in the bright polar summers, Ball explained.

When night falls on balloons launched from Texas or New Mexico, the gas inside cools and contracts. Unless they can drop nine hundred pounds at night, balloons descend and rarely stay aloft for more than a couple of days.

Pressurized, pumpkin-shaped, ultralong duration balloons may someday solve temperature and pressure problems in temperate climates. Until then, the twenty-four-hour sunlight of the polar summers provides a workable option. Balloons can fly for up to six weeks in that environment. But scientists do most of their preparatory work in Palestine, since trips to Antarctica get expensive.

The extreme ends of the earth give the recovery teams a whole new set of challenges.

"The secret of our universe's beginnings was being protected by caribou and polar bears," John Kageorge told the Associated Press in June 2005.

Kageorge was a spokesman for AMEC Dynamic Structures, Ltd., a company based in Port Coquitlam, British Columbia. It designed the Balloon-Borne Large Aperture Submillimeter Telescope, or BLAST, a device that detected microwaves generated billions of years ago. A team sent it up from NSBF's site in Sweden, and it landed four days later amid curious artic wildlife. The scientists on the recovery team armed themselves with rifles for protection.

Launches from Antarctica do not stand much chance of being mistaken for UFOs, considering that well-informed scientists can generally tell balloons from flying saucers and penguins do not seem to care. On the opposite side of the planet, few Swedes live inside the Artic Circle to spot the northern missions, and the lack of summer sunset robs the balloons of their fiery twilight glow.

Chapter 12:
The Skies over Sherman:
1898 and 1965

People named Campbell who live in Sherman, Texas, seem more likely than the average North Texan to see UFOs. Sixty-seven years apart, witnesses sharing that surname became key figures in publicly reported sightings in this Oklahoma-border town. A thorough search of well-organized obituary records at the Sherman Public Library revealed no conclusive evidence of blood relationship between the two, but the common name could imply an extended-family proclivity toward the fantastic.

"Great ball of fire"

Shortly after 9 p.m. on the evening of October 3, 1898, twelve-year-old George Campbell and his father, E.W., rode down what the locals called the "80-foot road," about two and half miles north of Sherman.

"All at once, everything got very bright," the youth told a Sherman *Register* reporter. "We saw a great ball of fire coming down toward the ground."

The object, which George estimated as measuring about ten feet across, steadily descended until it came within about three feet of land, then rose back into the sky. It emitted a buzzing sound that spooked the pair's horses. The *Register* journalist described the area of the sighting as depressed and swampy and the barometric pressure as low on the night in question.

That article praised young George as "a bright, intelligent little fellow who said he didn't believe in ghosts; that his parents had never scared him with spook stories and is one of the best behaved scholars in the Fourth grade at the Franklin school building." However, neither it nor a follow up story explained the apparent silence of George's father, who was also present on that nighttime ride.

Publication of George's story prompted other witnesses to come forward and corroborate it, among them Judge J.A.L. Wolfe and Grayson County attorney Silas Hare. The two men were traveling three to four miles west of Sherman the night George saw the fireball. They told the *Register* they also witnessed a steady light bright enough to read by.

"I involuntarily looked around for the electric light before I thought of the distance we were out of town," Judge Wolfe said. "There was a material difference between the light I noticed and the quick flash usually produced by a meteor."

Meanwhile, local teamster R.L. Leonard drove his horses southward into town on North Broughton, anxious to pass a lamp at College Street so he could sort out some jumbled papers. "All at once there was a bright light and it lasted until I had clearly discerned I had the looked-for paper in my hand. This light was north of me."

The October 6 issue of the *Register* also reprinted an account from the Dallas *Morning News* of strange lights seen concurrently in Garland. Its description of the "meteor" matched that given by Sherman witnesses but went further. After shooting back up into the air, the light burst into three colored spheres, one white, one bright blue, and the other bright red. "The red and blue lights soon died out, but the white one continued on its way a few seconds, when it burst, emitting a shower of stars which were extinguished almost immediately," the *News* reported.

163

August 1965

The Internet has made the other Campbell, one Robert L., perhaps the most enduring figure from a spate of sightings that stretched from Tulsa to Tucumcari during the first week of August 1965.

With NASA's Gemini tests in full swing, Earthlings had space and aeronautics on the brain that summer. Two months earlier, astronaut Edward H. White II became the first human to walk in space. And a news report from Fort Hood, Texas, chronicled the first "flawless test drop" of a model Gemini capsule. NASA eventually scrapped its goal for dry-ground landings instead of splashdowns for the Gemini, but in the summer of 1965, it dropped test modules from aircraft 12,200 feet in the air. They floated to the ground on red-and-white checked parasails that could be controlled like gliders. Developers rejoiced when a July 30 test landed only sixty yards from its target. Control malfunctions thwarted previous tests, the United Press International reported.

Mars also loomed large that summer. The Earth's relatively close orbital approach to Mars prompted the Americans and the Russians to launch exploratory craft. On July 14, Mariner IV began snapping pictures of the Red Planet. As one New York *Times* writer pointed out, if Martians wanted to overtake Earth, launching an invasion in the summer of 1965 would have shaved several million miles off their trip.

Space fed the imaginations of most Earthlings, like the trio of enterprising teenagers in Omaha, Nebraska, who successfully retrieved a live "moustronaut" after launching him on a two-and-a-half foot rocket from a vacant lot. Others took a more skeptical view of modern technology; ranchers in drought-stricken Carrizozo, New Mexico, blamed high-flying jets for chasing away rain clouds.

Meanwhile back in Sherman, a Dallas physician who specialized in space medicine explained to the Rotary Club how the space program and its spinoffs affected everyone in the country. "We are in a time of changing facts," Dr. Jim Maxfield told those assembled. "Facts now have become fiction and fiction has become facts. We are in a world of changing ideas. Medicine is going so fast that it is impossible for doctors to keep up."

As another two-man Gemini team prepared for a late August mission, the thoughts and gazes of mid-American's turned skyward.

An Oklahoma policeman spotted the first UFOs of that eventful week in the wee hours of Sunday, August 1. Officer Lewis Sikes told reporters he saw an object emitting red, white, and blue light hovering five miles northeast of Wynnewood, small town about half way between Oklahoma City and the Red River. The UFO remained visible for about forty-five minutes. Sikes claimed radar operators at Oklahoma's Tinker Air Force Base and at Carswell Air Force Base in Fort Worth tracked the object, which eventually disappeared about two miles south of Tinker. Yet no one aboard an airliner flying in the vicinity reported seeing anything unusual.

The following night, widely spread witnesses in Kansas, Oklahoma, Texas, and New Mexico saw all sorts of strange things in the sky. Policemen throughout the region described UFOs. Officers in three different patrol cars near Shawnee, Oklahoma, saw objects apparently flying in a diamond-shaped formation. The Wichita Weather Bureau in southern Kansas tracked an object that descended from 22,000 to 4,000 feet. The Oklahoma Highway Patrol reported that Tinker tracked as many as four UFOs by radar at even higher altitudes, but an official Tinker spokesman wouldn't confirm or deny those reports.

"The reported sightings this evening will be investigated by Air Force personnel," Lieutenant John Walmsley told the press.

Descriptions of UFOs sighted across the region varied, but many reports involved multicolored lights:

- Mr. and Mrs. Wayne Wirtz of Canyon saw three different UFOs while driving across the Panhandle from Greenville, New Mexico, to Dalhart, Texas. They alternately "exploded in a shower of sparks" and "fluttered like a leaf."
- A deputy sheriff in the Wirtz's hometown saw a similar spectacle. Dan Carter said the south-moving object "disintegrated in all colors." He at first mistook the UFO for an exploding aircraft.
- In Oklahoma, Patrolman C.V. Barnhill saw something kite-shaped topped by a red, revolving light.
- Mrs. Bill Tipton of Chandler, Oklahoma, claimed a white-on-top, red-on-bottom object hovered over the town for fifteen minutes, then shot off to the west.

Things really picked up after the sun went down on Sunday. That evening, the UFO party moved as far south as the Dallas–Fort Worth area, where switchboards lit up with hundreds of calls. Most reports involved lights of varying color. Mrs. Gerald Bostic told a different story—a buzzing, humming object hovered over her home and emitted a crystal-white light, she said.

One of the most spectacular accounts among the dozens of UFO sightings reported that night came from farther south, between Denton and Fort Worth. Two young men from Ponder said they saw "something silvery ease down into a field" near State Highway 156 between their hometown and Justin. Deputies from Denton and Tarrant counties investigated and found no evidence of a flying saucer landing. Two of them reported seeing something that looked like a magnesium flare near Justin, and another speculated that what they really spotted were headlights from a highway patrol car.

North Texans gave mixed reviews to the aerial light shows. The Denton *Record-Chronicle* interviewed citizens of that college town who offered varying opinions:

- "...space goes on and on and I guess you'll never know everything about it," mused Dude Roberson. "But it seems possible to me that there would be people out there."
- "All the rumors are a bunch of trash," surmised Amos Barksdale, citing experimental aircraft being developed in the area.
- "I wish it was the Air Force trying to invent something to scare all of the fight out of the Viet Cong. Not kill them, just scare them out of fighting," said Homer Edwards.
- "I try not to look at the sky; it might scare me to death," admitted William F. Derow.

Fuzzy Photos

At least four books recount the Sherman pair's early morning UFO chase, and a modern Internet compilation indiscriminately lifts text from all three without fact checking. For example, it repeats ufologist author Coral E. Lorenzen's mistake of placing the community of Bells in Oklahoma instead of Texas.

The books do not agree on the date of the escapade—it may have occurred early Monday morning or early Tuesday morning. They also offer conflicting information on McCollum's job title. Author Frank Edwards refers to him as a patrolman, while Lorenzen promotes him to chief of police.

The accounts do agree that the two met up about 3 a.m. after listening to police radio traffic about UFOs. They drove around Bells, a small town five or six miles east of Sherman, and Campbell snapped a few black-and-white still shots of something in the sky. Ufologists carefully chronicle the exact type of camera and film Campbell used to capture an indefinable blur in a two-minute time exposure.

The man behind many of the Air Force's scientific explanations for UFOs—astrophysicist J. Allen Hynek of Northwestern University—later visited Sherman himself and interviewed Campbell. Hynek had served as Project Blue Book's chief scientific advisor since 1952 and was often quoted when odd things appeared in the sky. However, he bristled at the suggestion that his analyses rubberstamped military propaganda. Many flying objects remained unidentified not because they represented true scientific puzzles but because of inadequate Air Force follow up, Hynek frequently complained. Hynek became even more skeptical of some of the Air Force's pat answers after a puzzling incident involving a peace officer in Socorro, New Mexico, that both he and Lorenzen investigated in 1964.

Hynek carefully categorized UFOs, popularizing the "close encounter" nomenclature. He included Campbell's light-blob photo in his 1972 book, *The UFO Experience: A Scientific Inquiry*, and classified the Sherman incident as an atypical nocturnal lights sighting. During his visit to North Texas, Hynek had Campbell use the same camera to take pictures of streetlights for comparison. "I had no cause to suspect a hoax," the scientist wrote.

Perhaps local journalistic rivalry kept word of Campbell's photo out of the Sherman *Democrat*; the newspaper relied mostly on wire stories to cover the August UFO flap. Its original reporting consisted of a few short paragraphs quoting a couple of local witnesses—including county clerk's office employee Harry Edens—and relaying the official "no comment" from the city's Perrin Air Force Base. A feature the following Sunday on manifestations of the "silly season" dropped a passing mention of flying saucers while devoting paragraphs to teenage fads such as toenail art, wooden rings, slot-car racing, skateboarding, and wearing shoes without socks. Najeeb E. Halaby, a former Federal Aviation Administration director, seemed to agree with the *Democrat's* assessment. "Reports of such objects seem to peak in August and September. It may be that the long, hot summer expedites the imagination," said Halaby, who also indicated the rash of sightings might signal the rise of a new "American mythology."

Elsewhere, however, Campbell's picture obviously got plenty of attention. The same Sunday that the Sherman *Democrat* dismissed flying saucers as silliness, the New York *Times* referenced the shot in a news-of-the-week wrap up. "A TV newsman in Sherman, Tex., produced a photograph of something that looked like an explosion," it reported.

A Tulsa teenager captured another semifamous UFO image from his backyard that week. The Oklahoma City *Journal* ran 14-year-old Alan R. Smith's photo on its front page in October after studying the negative and declaring it genuine. The U.S. Air Force Photo Analysis Division agreed the photo showed some material object but noted its similarity to photos of "a multicolored revolving filter flood light."

Saucer Chasers

By Tuesday night, a small contingent from the Dallas/Fort Worth media decided to go aloft to solve the mystery. Pilot Bill Hoover of Mustang Aviation took WFAA-TV meteorologist Dale Milford, Dallas *Morning News* reporter Kent Biffle, and photographer Fred Coston up in a Piper Aztec to chase UFOs.

A two-hundred-foot-thick temperature inversion blanketed the region, Milford noted. Biffle described the hazy layer of air as "a ghostly gray island floating across miles of sky, and full of dull radiance captured from light of nearby cities." The inversion appeared most notable northeast of Dallas.

As the group ascended, they fixed their attention on a star underneath the Little Dipper that seemed to jump up and down and flicker in a variety of colors. But once they rose above the inversion layer, the star stopped its dance and remained fixed and constant.

The newsmen crisscrossed the Metroplex for hours, following tips from WFAA reporters chasing UFOs on the ground. From above, they never found anything interesting except the inversion layer filtering and distorting light and radio signals below. At one point, they realized people on the ground were reporting lights from their own aircraft as a UFO.

In 1969, a team led by scientist Edward Uhler Condon prepared a government-issued report intended by some to be the official last word on UFOs. The Condon report reinforced the saucer-chasers' observations. It addressed the spate of sightings by focusing on a UFO seen near Wichita, Kansas, in the early morning hours of August 2. Researchers noted a marked temperature inversion recorded at Topeka and in Oklahoma City. Condon attributed visual and radar anomalies to a warm layer of air at a high altitude.

Inevitably, the spate of sightings inspired a couple of good stories from farmers with penchants for tall tales or loose perceptions of reality. Reports of a flying saucer landing in a pasture southeast of Fort Worth near Kennedale on the night of Biffle's flight turned out to be a hoax. And one farmer in Dallas County told the Air Force that Russian planes often used his barn as an "aiming point" toward Carswell. He promised to take a picture the next time it flew over.

The Official Verdict

Four decades of reporting on the more interesting aspects of life in North Texas now muddle Biffle's memory of his adventures that night. He does recall that the same edition of the *News* that chronicled his UFO chase included a wire story on page 9-A relaying the official federal position on the phenomena. By then, Major Hector Quintanilla Jr., a 42-year-old physicist, had taken the reigns of the Project Blue Book program. Temperature inversions gave a "scintillating effect" to four prominent stars and the planet Jupiter, he said.

However, the official government explanation seemed ludicrous to some witnesses.

"They can stop kidding us now about there being no such thing as 'flying saucers,' " stated a Fort Worth *Star-Telegram* editorial. "Too many people of obviously sound mind saw and reported them independently from too many separate localities. Their descriptions of what they saw were too similar to one another, and too unlike any familiar object.

"And it's going to take more than a statistical report on how many reported 'saucers' have turned out to be weather balloons to convince us otherwise."

The rash of sightings also added to Hynek's growing doubts. And in March 1966, he would be lampooned by the press for offering swamp gas as a possible explanation for a spate of fast-moving UFOs seen by more than two hundred people in Michigan. After the closure of Project Blue Book, Hynek founded the Center for UFO Studies, a restrained but open-minded investigative organization.

In October 1966, *Newsweek* published an interview with Dr. Hynek.

"There is a phenomenon here. I've studied this for eighteen years and it's not all nonsense," Hynek said. "I'm not saying we are being visited by extraterrestrial beings, but I believe it is one of the possibilities, and I think we should hold an open mind about it. It would be provincial to believe we are the only intelligent beings in the universe."

Chapter 13:
Friday Night Lights:
Damon, Texas, September 1965

Eighty-one-year-old Billy McCoy remembers it like it was yesterday. What he saw that late-summer night in 1965 changed his whole perspective on the universe.

Neither he nor fellow witness Bob Goode were men to be trifled with back then. McCoy had earned the first letter jacket Freeport High School ever awarded for boxing. He won several Golden Globe tournaments in Houston, then fought professionally for several years in the late 1940s and early '50s. Boxing injuries disqualified McCoy for military service, although he tried to join more than once. The violent career of his youth left him with a glass eye, a perforated eardrum, and several large, gnarly knuckles.

The older of the pair, Goode served in the Army during World War II and earned two Bronze Stars. He became a career law enforcement officer afterward. McCoy once saw a nefarious type stick a cocked gun into Goode's belly. Goode jammed a finger between the hammer and firing pin and proceeded to knock the fellow down.

"He wasn't afraid of the devil himself," McCoy said, "and [what happened in 1965] this scared the devil out of him."

By then, both had become well-respected members of the Brazoria County Sheriff's Office. Many considered their credibility unassailable.

The chief deputy's position came with a few perks. For McCoy, then thirty-eight, these included the excuse to provide crowd control when high schools met to settle rivalries on the football field. On Friday, September 3, that meant driving over to Sweeny for the big game against West Columbia.

There, McCoy ran into Goode, who was officially on duty at the game that night though nursing a sore finger. Just before leaving his home, a baby alligator snapped as Goode tried to free it from a tub in his garage. Figuring the only doctor in town would be at the game, Goode bandaged a bleeding finger on his left hand and headed for the stadium. McCoy noticed the red inflammation streaking down Goode's hand and agreed when the fifty-year-old deputy asked for company on his nightly patrols after the game. Goode ostensibly feared his injury might become too painful for driving, but McCoy thinks the older deputy may have just wanted someone to talk to during his lonely rounds of ranch roads in the western part of the county.

More than Lights

The pair cruised the few streets in the small community of Damon, not far from the Fort Bend County line, shortly before 11 p.m. Goode then turned his Chevrolet interceptor south down State Highway 36. The pair eased along at thirty to forty miles an hour, chatting and enjoying the clear night and bright moon. Crossing a flat prairie a few miles outside of Damon, McCoy spotted unusual lights that most definitely did not emanate from a football stadium.

"It looked like a purple light, just flashing over there, and I said something to Bob about it," McCoy told researcher Colleen Kenyon in a 1985 oral history interview. Gas wells dotted the landscape, and the pair at first thought they might be seeing a mercury vapor light on a pump station.

Goode kept driving until McCoy saw a smaller blue light emerge from the purple one. Goode parked the car on the roadside, and both got out for a better look. As they watched, the blue light moved and stopped twice more along a horizontal plane. "The brilliant purple light and the little blue light just floated up in the air eight or ten degrees above the horizon, and just hung there," McCoy said. Both lights appeared vertically oblong.

The lights seemed to be a few miles away, in the direction of the San Bernard River. The two got in their car and backtracked toward Damon, intending to find a river road and get a closer look. But Goode stopped less than a mile down the highway and stuck his binoculars out the window.

"When he put his binoculars up to look at the thing, it was in an instant right on top of us," McCoy said in a 2008 interview.

The purple light filled the car, and Goode felt heat on the arm and hand he had crooked out he window. This close, the men could see that the lights were attached to something—a solid gray object that looked as long as a football field, forty to fifty feet thick in the middle. It hovered near the car, about 100 to 150 feet in the air. But at the time, documenting the object's dimensions was not a priority for Goode and McCoy.

"Ol' Bob, he showered down on the gas pedal, and we took off from there just as fast as that police interceptor would go," McCoy recalled. "I don't know why we thought we could outrun it. If it wanted to catch us, all it would had to do was just swoop down on us."

McCoy watched the object as Goode barreled toward Damon. Grass and trees beneath the UFO appeared undisturbed as it moved back toward the river at a slower pace, then shot straight up at a ninety-degree angle.

The men stopped in Damon and puffed on cigarettes to steady their nerves. They set out again, hoping to discover what the object was.

McCoy and Goode saw nothing as they traveled along the back roads, through wild country near the river. But when they returned to Highway 36, the lights appeared again.

Brazoria County deputies Bob Goode and Billy McCoy were patrolling this area southeast of Damon, Texas, when they spotted a UFO over a field near the San Bernard River bottoms. (Photo courtesy of Renee Roderick.)

This time, the men decided to seek help from some reputable folks in West Columbia, including a city judge with an interest in UFOs. However, the object gave no repeat performance when they returned with more potential witnesses.

The deputies gave up the UFO hunt by 3 or 4 a.m. and stopped at a bowling alley for breakfast. They tried to make some sense of the night while sipping coffee and eating scrambled eggs. McCoy noticed Goode using his bandaged finger without complaint.

" 'One good thing about this,' I said, '[it] made you forget about your finger hurting,' " McCoy recounted. "He said, 'Well, that thing isn't sore.' "

Goode removed his bandage to find the swelling and redness gone. The finger looked practically unharmed by the next day.

Strange Little Men at the Café

Word of the deputies' close encounter spread throughout the county and beyond within a few days. But before the story ever made headlines, a couple of unusual visitors showed up in county seat trying to find McCoy and Goode.

The chief deputy was out of town on Sunday, September 5, when the strangers came looking for him at the sheriff's office in Angleton. They also asked for Goode, so the dispatcher radioed the on-duty deputy to arrange a meeting.

The pair stood out so that Goode spotted them immediately when they walked into the Twin Oaks Café in West Columbia. Goode would later describe them as small and Asian looking, wearing dark suits and derby hats. Being the only law enforcement officer in the restaurant made Goode equally hard to miss.

The men introduced themselves as reporters from Pasadena but offered no business cards. "They started telling *him* what had happened to *us*," McCoy said.

The odd visitors told Goode that if the deputies had not been afraid, they would have been taken for a ride in the UFO and returned to their car unharmed. But if the deputies ever told anyone about the wonders they saw, the men in black warned they would return and make "jabbering idiots" out of them.

That night, Goode called McCoy, worried about what the out-of-towners had said.

"I said, 'Well, Bob, we don't have anything to worry about, 'cause we didn't stop, we didn't go for a ride on it,' " McCoy said. " 'Some people might think we are jabbering idiots anyway.' "

Goode couldn't remember the men's names, but the deputies tried to figure out where the visitors came from. They called newspapers and radio stations in every town in the country called Pasadena—not just the ship channel city forty miles to the north. None of the media outlets admitted sending reporters to Brazoria County.

"So we don't know where those people come from, or who they were. Don't know what happened to them," McCoy said.

Investigations

Word began to circulate about the deputies' experience, and along with pranksters, several serious callers phoned the sheriff's office to admit seeing similar objects in the area as far back as the mid-1950s, the Angleton *Times* would report.

The night after their sighting, Goode and McCoy returned to the same spot on Highway 36 with reinforcements, including a Texas Department of Public Safety sergeant and an identification officer who stood by with cameras. The UFO failed to make an encore appearance that night or the next two.

The following Wednesday, Houston's Ellington Air Force Base sent Major Laurence R. Leach out. He filed his final report with the Foreign Technology Division at Wright-Patterson Air Force base in Ohio within a week of his visit to Brazoria County. The Air Force team's Geiger counters found no radiation in the pasture, on the car, or on Goode's left shirtsleeve, although Leach's report noted that rain fell twice between the sighting and his investigation. The Houston Air Traffic Control Center found no flight plans spanning the area for the night in question and no unusual radar reports, although anything below 2,000 feet would not have registered on radar. Weather data indicated a temperature inversion, but the Air Force for once did not attempt to pin the deputies' sighting on that common UFO explanation.

The major also determined McCoy and Goode to be credible witnesses, according to his report:

After talking with both officers involved in the sighting, there is no doubt in my mind that they definitely saw some unusual object or phenomenon. However, my investigation failed to uncover any facts that permitted me … to arrive at an explanation for the unusual sighting.

Both officers appeared to be intelligent, mature, levelheaded and persons capable of sound judgment and reasoning. Chief Deputy Sheriff McCoy holds a responsible position in the department requiring the supervision of over 42 personnel.

Both officers have been subjected to considerable friendly ridicule from their contemporaries and the local townspeople; but, have continued to profess the facts of their sighting.

"As far as I know, our sighting is still on the books as a documented UFO sighting that they haven't been able to explain," McCoy said.

A Sighting Back East
The same date Billy McCoy and Bob Goode spotted a UFO hovering near the San Bernard River bottoms, an unexplained object appeared to another pair of law enforcement officers, this one a few miles inland from the Atlantic Coast. Ultimately, the sighting near Exeter, New Hampshire, overshadowed the Damon incident in the annals of UFO history, perhaps because more people were around to see it.

The 1960s marked the peak of activity for nearby Pease Air Force Base. The Air Force took over an airport previously controlled by the Navy in 1951 to establish Pease as a base for the Strategic Air Command. From midnight to 2 a.m. on September 3, flyers from the base conducted exercises in the area codenamed "Operation Big Bang." Air Force investigators would attribute the sightings to B-47s sent aloft for the exercise, and/or to astronomic phenomena. But the UFO reports began just as the exercises were wrapping up and continued for an hour or more.

The first report came from a female motorist who told a police officer that a large object followed her for several miles as she drove between New England towns. It would soon appear around 2 a.m. to a teenage hitchhiker who then caught a ride to the Exeter police station. He brought an officer back to the field where he had seen the object, and another patrolman joined them when the craft reappeared.

The Exeter object shared some similarities with the one McCoy and Goode spotted in Brazoria County—it was large, lighted, silent, and low flying. But unlike the Texas UFO, the one in New Hampshire flashed a series of red lights in a sequence. Witnesses said those lights shone so brightly they could not make out the object's shape. And instead of moving smoothly like the Damon craft, the Exeter object fluttered like a leaf as it appeared and disappeared from behind trees and buildings.

According to ufologist J. Allen Hynek's analysis of Project Blue Book documentation, the two police officers took offense to the Air Force's summary dismissal of their sighting. They wrote Project Blue Book commander Major Hector Quintanilla Jr. twice imploring him to put something in writing refuting the Pentagon's public statement on the issue.

"...as you might imagine, we have been the subject of considerable ridicule since the Pentagon released its 'final evaluation' of our sighting of September 3, 1965," Eugene Bertrand wrote on behalf of himself and fellow patrolman David Hunt. "Since our job depends on accuracy and the ability to tell the difference between fact and fiction, we were naturally disturbed by the report the Pentagon issued which attributed the sighting to 'multiple high-altitude objects in the area' and 'weather inversion.' "

Eventually, Bertrand and Hunt received some semblance of the response they sought in a letter from the Office of the Secretary of the Air Force. Although it stated that investigations of more than ten thousand UFO reports over nearly two decades "proved almost conclusively" that such sightings can be attributed to manmade objects or to atmospheric or astronomic phenomena, it allowed that "based on additional information submitted to our UFO Investigation Officer, Wright-Patterson AFB, Ohio, we have been unable to identify the object that you observed."

UFO People

Unlike their law-enforcement counterparts in New Hampshire, McCoy and Goode experienced no overt derision from the Air Force following their sighting. In fact, because of his experience and his willingness to discuss it, McCoy crossed paths over the years with famous and infamous ufologists. UFO clubs from all over invited the deputies to their meetings, and they obliged several within driving distance of Brazoria County. McCoy found some investigators to be serious and scientific, and others just plain weird. For instance, one guy cornered him during a refreshment break at a meeting in Houston. The fellow asked McCoy if he would like to speak to the people in the craft he saw.

"I said, 'Yeah, I think I really would.' "

"He said, 'Well, let me tell you how to do it.' He said, 'Some dark night if you'll just drive off out in the middle of a pasture somewhere, get away from the city lights, just get you a lawn chair and you sit out there and you concentrate real hard on that space craft. Just ask them—'Make contact. Make contact.' " (McCoy chanted that last part, and then chuckled.)

"I said, 'Boy, that's all we need down in Brazoria County…a deputy sheriff to be caught out there in a local pasture with his badge on saying, 'Make contact.' "

McCoy's first brush with the UFO elite came just ten days after his sighting. Al Chop flew down to Houston to appear on a late-night local television show hosted on KRPC by Ray Miller. Chop, the Air Force spokesman who was chummy with UFO zealot and military irritant Donald Keyhoe, appeared on the program with McCoy and Hugh Alexander, an assistant professor of space science at Rice University.

"We had a good roundtable discussion," McCoy recalled. "[But Chop] didn't say anything on TV that would jeopardize his job."

Off camera, however, Chop said plenty. He talked of a military plane that had scrambled over Lake Superior to intercept a UFO. Radar watched as the plane and the object appeared to merge, then disappeared. Neither was ever found despite extensive searches.

The incident Chop referred to occurred November 23, 1953. Radar operators observed unidentified blips in restricted air space over Soo Locks near Sault Ste. Marie. Here, Lake Superior begins spilling along the Michigan/Ontario border into Lake Huron. First Lieutenant Felix Moncla and Second Lieutenant Robert Wilson took off in an F-89 from an Air Force base in nearby Kincheloe, Michigan, at 6:22 p.m., and their plane dropped off radar about half an hour later. Canadian prospectors claimed to find the wreckage in 1968, and a dive company temporarily posted a similar claim on the Internet in 2006, but neither group provided any credible evidence of its location.

"[Chop] told several things like that, but then he sat right there [on camera] and said, 'I don't believe that we are being visited by alien beings because…we would have some physical evidence in our hand by this time."

McCoy and Goode also soon became acquainted with J. Allen Hynek. The noted astrophysicist had been Project Blue Book's original chief scientific advisor, but by the mid-1960s had become increasingly frustrated about the Air Force's inadequate and dismissive UFO investigations. Although Hynek did not visit Brazoria County personally, he spoke with both men several times by phone to investigate the incident.

"Professor Hynek was so sure that what we saw was a UFO because of that 90-degree turn it made," McCoy said.

The deputies' sighting occurred during a national UFO flap that proved a turning point for Hynek. Highlights of this space-age spate of UFO appearances included the fuzzy photos taken in Sherman, the Damon and Exeter sightings, and a rash of reports in Michigan in the spring of 1966. These events brought about what Hynek hoped would mark true progress in the field of UFO research—they forced the Air Force and Congress to acknowledge the need for a more serious investigation.

This led to the formation of the official UFO study group led by Dr. Edward U. Condon. Dr. James McDonald of Arizona strongly believed Keyhoe's extraterrestrial hypothesis and badly wanted to serve on the committee. When Condon snubbed him, McDonald turned his energies toward fomenting dissent among committee members. He also lobbied sympathetic Congressmen and managed to schedule a hearing before the House Committee on Space and Aeronautics. McDonald asked McCoy and Goode to attend the July 29, 1968 hearing, but the pair declined since no one offered to pay their travel expenses. However, their sighting did come up during the hearing.

"He said they were trying to explain ours away as being a reflection of the star Antares," McCoy said. "Professor McDonald had said that [because of] the time of our sighting and the position of the earth in relation to Antares, that this was an impossibility and he wanted to prove it."

More Witnesses, More UFOS

The mid-'60s wave of UFO sightings continued into the next year, with witnesses across the country reporting not only strange lights, but sometimes substantial machinery attached to them. In February and March 1966, a pair of Texans hundred of miles apart compared the shapes of the UFOs they saw to aquatic creatures.

The first sighting occurred about 115 miles northeast of the Brazoria County incident location and nearly as far inland from the Gulf of Mexico. Project Blue Book dismissed it as "psychological," an easy explanation when only one person admits seeing something particularly unusual. The incident happened in Nederland, a community between Beaumont and Port Arthur near the Louisiana state line. Hynek published an account in 1977 but deleted the witness's name to protect his privacy.

On February 6, a Nederland man and his wife woke up about 5:45 a.m. as their son passed through their bedroom on the way to the bathroom. The lights then flashed off, and the gentleman went outside to see if the power outage affected the entire neighborhood. It did. But some other light source cast a pulsating red glow across the yard.

Like the Exeter policemen, the Nederland witness reported seeing a craft adorned with a horizontal lights that flashed in sequence. The UFO also flew low, about five hundred feet from the ground. The craft seemed silent, but the witness and his wife sensed a very high-frequency tone.

The witness estimated the craft's initial position as a couple of miles west of the Jefferson County Airport. He also saw a conventional aircraft take off and fly toward the UFO. (Hynek's account, taken from Project Blue Book files, does not indicate whether the chaser was a fixed-wing plane or a helicopter.) The mysterious object extinguished its own lights as the terrestrial aircraft flew over it, but the witness made out the UFO's shape in lights shining beneath the aircraft. He compared it with a tadpole, noting a six-foot, lighted tail extending from a main body about eight-feet in diameter. Soon the object disappeared, flying slowly to the west.

As with many UFO witnesses, the Nederland resident feared going public with the story. However, he chatted with an electric company employee in the neighborhood the next day, who attributed the power outage to transformer failure.[1]

Eddie Laxson, a fifty-six-year-old civilian instructor at Sheppard Air Force Base in Wichita Falls, got an even closer look at a UFO on March 23. Hynek also wrote about the Laxson sighting, drawing heavily from a Dallas *Times-Herald* article published four days later.

Driving on U.S. Highway 70 on the Oklahoma side of the Red River, Laxson encountered what he at first thought was a large vehicle or house-moving rig stopped in the road with red lights flashing. Thinking mechanical problems likely, Laxson pulled over to help.

As he walked closer to the apparently stranded vehicle, he saw something he could not explain. The seventy-five-foot-long object looked like a wingless military aircraft, complete with a Plexiglas bubble. Laxson compared it to a perch (a small freshwater fish often gutted, scaled, and fried whole, or used as bait on catfish trotlines). He then saw a man wearing what looked like a mechanic's cap climb into the craft from the far side and take off amid a great hissing sound.

Laxson at first decided not to discuss what he saw, but about a mile down the road, he came upon another witness, C.W. Anderson, a driver for Magnum Oil and Gas Company. Anderson watched the light from the craft whiz along the Red River, just a few miles to the southeast.

As the Nederland and Wichita Falls tales indicate, reporting UFOs grew increasingly taboo as the '60s drew to a close.

---

[1] Some researchers posit that UFOs may have been responsible for a series of mysterious, wide-scale power outages that affected the United States, England, and Argentina during the last two months of 1965. This wave began with the Great Northeast Blackout in early November that left 36 million people in the dark.

"It takes more courage to report a thing like this than it does to forget it," Laxson told the press. "I know that people will say that Laxson is durned crazy. But that's what I saw."

Ufologists surmise that the fear of becoming local laughingstocks kept many witnesses from talking about things they saw in the sky. This may very well be the case in Brazoria County. Over the years, several people approached McCoy and local historians with whispered accounts of UFO sightings, but few were willing to subject themselves to public ridicule.

A couple of years go, one fellow dropped into the packing shop McCoy's son Kevin then owned. He told Kevin he saw the same thing the deputies did on September 3, 1965, from a vantage point in the San Bernard river bottoms. He had a valid reason for not coming forward—fear of prosecution. He and a couple of buddies were hunting out of season and were afraid of being arrested if they publicly supported McCoy's story.

Making Sense of It All

Goode worked for the sheriff's department for twenty-four years, served a stint as West Columbia's chief of police, and retired after a dozen years as a justice of the peace in that community. He eventually tired of talking about UFOs and refused all interview requests in his later years. Goode died in January 2001.

McCoy left the sheriff's department less than a year after the sighting, seeking a less demanding and more lucrative way to support his family. He worked in the construction industry and later owned an antique shop. He still helps run that packaging materials business in Lake Jackson, even though Kevin sold it a few years ago to a larger company.

Unlike Goode, McCoy never completely put the UFO experience behind him. He took in stride the occasional late-night calls from drunks reporting wife-flung flying saucers. Some critics asked why McCoy and Goode did not take a picture of or fire shots at the object. McCoy explained that if the pair had had a camera, they would have been too frightened to use it. And why shoot at something when you do not know its intentions?

The tale also continues to gather attention from ufologists worldwide. The Sci-Fi Channel reenacted it for a program in the late 1990s, and a researcher in Iowa called McCoy in 2007. She was helping a friend in Italy, who was writing a UFO book in his native language.

Through the years, McCoy has never regretted the sighting, and he never tried to hide it.

"I guess it's the same way if a person's pretty secure in how they feel about God. They're not ashamed to talk about it, you know," McCoy said in the oral history interview. "I don't feel any worse for having seen it. I don't necessarily feel any better for having seen all of it....[W]hat we are is a total sum of all of our experiences, and I guess if anything, that I just feel like that's one experience that the majority didn't have, so I guess it helped me see things a little differently."

Not that McCoy considered the UFO sighting a religious experience, like one fellow he met at a UFO club meeting. That true believer described alien visitors as wayward souls from other planets looking for a place to spend eternity. McCoy chuckles and shakes his head at that notion, but he does not believe the idea of visitors from outer space conflicts with Christianity.

"It doesn't destroy the theory that God created the Earth and everything therein," McCoy mused. "There's no reason that someone else couldn't be out there."

Make no mistake—McCoy is a believer, in God and in intelligence from other worlds.

"I believe we have been visited for a long time. I don't think they mean any harm to us. I think they are as curious about us as we are about them," McCoy said. He suspects that human violence and jealousy discourage extraterrestrials from making contact or sticking around. "People who are looking for peace just wouldn't want to be here."

Billy McCoy, 81, spends most days helping run a packaging materials business founded by his son in Lake Jackson. He frankly and cheerfully answers questions from the occasional researcher about the UFO he and fellow deputy Bob Goode encountered near Damon on September 3, 1965. (Photo courtesy Renee Roderick.)

CHAPTER 14:
CLOSE ENCOUNTER OF THE
EAST TEXAS KIND:
HUFFMAN, 1980

The most defining characteristic of an unidentified flying object is the "unidentified" part. Once an unassailable explanation surfaces—flares tied to helium balloons by a Phoenix prankster, for example—a flying object ceases to be unidentified.

In the early 1950s, the U.S. Air Force estimated that when subjected to close investigation, more than 90 percent of UFOs lost the "U." The remaining 10 percent or less created enough uncertainty to spawn countless urban—and in this case rural— legends.

One flying object that remains unidentified nearly three decades after its sighting reportedly hovered over the treetops on the edge of the East Texas Pincy Woods.

Historically, people who didn't want to be found often sought cover in the dense forests and secluded swamps of Southeast Texas. In such environs, concepts like Big Foot and ghost lights seem a little less alien than they might in the concrete jungles of nearby Houston.

Farm Road 1485 may have been a narrow stretch of pavement cutting a lonely path through the forest in 1980. But as is the case with so many other Texas byways, 21st century development now leaves this two-lane thoroughfare overtaxed and outdated. "Farm Road" now seems a quaint designation to suburbanites without tractors. Turning east from New Caney, a Sunday driver encounters moderately heavy traffic on the north side of Lake Houston State Park. Firewood stands and auto repair shops gradually give way to billboards and small roadside signs advertising builders and housing developments. Traffic then lightens past Huffman, and Farm Road 1485 becomes truly rural for the last several miles to Dayton.

This stretch of Farm Road 1485 was even more isolated in December 1980, when Betty Cash stopped her new Cutlass Supreme in the middle of it to avoid driving under a fire-belching UFO. She and her passengers, Vickie and Colby Landrum, never discovered its origin. (Photo courtesy of Renee Roderick.)

A few sections of the road remain shoulderless, including the stretch identified in several accounts as the area where three Dayton residents reported a close encounter on December 29,

1980. Here, Farm Road 1485 has made a ninety-degree right turn to the south. Hidden behind a wall of pines to the west lies a burgeoning neighborhood of upscale mini-estates with white wooden fences surrounding stone-and-brick homes, some of them boasting multicar garages. A tall communications tower on the east side of the road keeps urban-refugee homeowners in cell-phone contact with their Houston interests.

Bingo Denied

The new Cutlass Supreme Betty Cash drove in 1980 probably didn't come equipped with one of the clunky, car-tethered mobile phones of the day. And even if it had, the phone would have been of little use as she and two friends returned from an unsuccessful bingo game quest two nights before New Year's Eve.

The recently divorced Cash, fifty-one, planned to open a new restaurant in a few days. Her friend Vickie Landrum, fifty-seven, worked for Cash as a waitress and was raising her seven-year-old grandson, Colby, who went along for the ride.

Holiday disruptions to their usual routines left the trio a bit disoriented. Thinking it was a Tuesday night instead of a Monday, they first headed to Cleveland, a larger community to the northwest on Highway 59. They found their usual bingo hall dark that night, attributing this at first to a holiday schedule change. Likewise, they found closed doors after driving on to New Caney looking for another game. Giving up on bingo, the three pulled in to a truck stop before heading back to Dayton. Cash sipped a cup of coffee while the Landrums enjoyed a late meal.

When the small group piled back into Cash's car, she turned on the heater to ward off the winter chill. A dozen miles down Farm Road 1485, Cash and the Landrums began seeing lights they assumed belonged to aircraft preparing to land at Houston Intercontinental Airport. But soon, what they spied hovering above two-lane road near Huffman made Cash stop in her tracks.

The women later told authorities they encountered some kind of aircraft hovering atop the tall pines that lined the rural road. The women estimated the object—shaped like a blunt-edged diamond and ringed with small blue lights—to be about the size of Dayton's water tower.

Fear of the flames issuing from beneath the craft prompted Cash to stop in the middle of the road. In a taped interview the following August at Austin's Bergstrom Air Force Base, Cash told officials her car went dead. "I mean, it was like somebody had turned a switch off on it," she said.

The two women exited the car, but Mrs. Landrum soon got back inside to comfort her frightened grandson.

"He was screaming and crying and everything so, and I thought the world was coming to an end," she told the acting judge advocate at Bergstrom. "I was telling him to look right inside. If he saw a big man, it'd be Jesus…. I was trying to keep him quiet and show him something that would be more pleasant than what he was seein'."

The craft settled down over the trees between bursts of fire, which sent it higher in the sky, the women said. This went on for ten minutes or more before the object began moving away to the southwest.

Cash got back into her now operable car and turned on the air conditioner. Intense heat from the UFO's flame forced Cash to wrap her leather jacket around her hand to open the car door. Inside the vehicle, she claimed Mrs. Landrum's palm left an impression in her heat-softened dashboard.

The would-be bingo players then noticed the helicopters.

By the early 1980s, black helicopters had become part of UFO folklore. People who reported seeing unidentified spacecraft often also saw twin-rotor military choppers. The occasional UFO witness also reported subsequent harassment by threatening, mysterious men wearing black suits and driving black cars.

"The helicopters were on both sides of it and looked like they were trying their best to get around the top of it. It was unreal," Cash told the Air Force.

Cash sped away but pulled over at a highway intersection a few miles down the road to get a better look at the helicopters. She and Landrum counted more than twenty of them flying along with the UFO but admitted that their tally could have been off since the helicopters moved around so much. The Air Force officials at Bergstrom would later grill the women about the precise wording on the helicopters, with Cash insisting the words "United States Air Force" marked their sides.

As they traveled on to Dayton, the three promised each other they wouldn't talk about what they saw for fear of public ridicule. Cash took the Landrums home shortly before 10 p.m., then drove to her own house. Within hours, all three fell ill.

Unexplained Illness

Cash, who had spent the most time outside the vehicle during the UFO encounter, experienced the harshest symptoms—headaches, nausea, diarrhea, red skin, and knots that turned into blisters. The Landrums felt sunburned and experienced gastrointestinal distress and eye problems.

Mrs. Landrum eventually brought Cash to her home to better care for both her friend and Colby. Cash's condition continued to deteriorate, so Landrum took her to a Houston hospital. Cash spent the better part of the next month there, losing much of her hair and patches of skin. Her illness perplexed physicians. The women eventually came clean about their strange encounter after Colby blurted that "that thing we saw" must have made Cash sick.

"I laid in that hospital and suffered that thirteen days before I would even level with my doctor, 'cause I didn't want anybody to think I was crazy," Cash said at Bergstrom. " 'Cause I had never believed in things like this. But it definitely didn't have little green men with pointed ears."

Because Cash delayed revealing her UFO encounter, her physicians could not say whether it caused her illness. Houston radiologist Dr. James Easley examined the women six months later, but too much time had passed by then to definitively link their health problems to radiation exposure.

Cash, who never fully regained her health, spent most of her remaining years in Birmingham, Alabama, in the care of her mother. Her physician there, Dr. Byran McClelland, told the Houston *Chronicle* that Cash suffered radiation poisoning equivalent to what a nuclear bomb survivor would have experienced "three to five miles from the epicenter of Hiroshima."

UFO skeptics scoffed at McClelland's assertion, claiming that victims of a radiation dose intense enough to cause almost immediate symptoms would not live more than a few days to tell the tale. Others suggested possible exposure to toxic chemicals.

Whatever caused their illnesses, Mrs. Landrum and her grandson completely agreed with Cash's opinion of the aircraft's origin.

"It had to be manmade," Mrs. Landrum said in Austin.

"Uh huh...why do you say it had to be manmade?" Captain John Camp asked.

"Well I don't think...there are any little green men out there to make one," she replied.

A strange conversation with an Army National Guard pilot several months after the UFO incident seemed to support their suspicion of military involvement.

Dayton is a rodeo town, and the local Future Farmer's of America chapter hosted its annual livestock show and rodeo on April 30, 1981. The CH-47 helicopter that landed for public display in a vacant lot proved to be a popular attraction. UFO researcher and mechanical engineer John F. Schuessler, a McDonnell-Douglas space-flight project manager, had by this time begun investigating the Huffman sighting. When Mrs. Landrum spotted the chopper flying over the town, she immediately called a friend to help her track it town. She then called Schuessler, who advised her to get the pilot's name and ask as many questions as possible.

Mrs. Landrum and Colby stood in line to tour the aircraft along with their friend, Martha Thompson. Thompson brought along a scrap of paper and planned to have the pilot write down his name under the guise of getting his autograph for her son. The plan worked, and when Mrs. Landrum mentioned having seen just such a helicopter on December 29, the pilot told them his unit had been called out that night by the Montgomery County Sheriff's Department. But after Mrs. Landrum exclaimed that she had been injured by a UFO, the pilot abruptly turned his attention to others waiting to see the helicopter.

The group maintained their belief in the UFO's worldly—and probably military—origin, but they clearly overcame their aversion to talking about the incident, at least for the next several years. Their story appeared in the *Weekly World News* and the Houston *Chronicle*, and Mrs. Landrum was hypnotized on a 1981 episode of *That's Incredible!* And they told the Air Force officers at Bergstrom that after leaving the base that day, they planned to visit a radio station to listen to a variety of recorded sounds in an effort to identify the beeping and whooshing noises the UFO made.

Their story remained consistent in repeated retellings, and the trio's willingness to publicly discuss their experience seemed to embolden other witnesses to come forward with their own accounts. Schuessler interviewed several of people who saw something on December 29, 1980. He included their accounts in articles and a book he later wrote, and he discussed them with the Houston *Chronicle*:

- Angie Stanley, a twenty-six-year-old postal clerk, saw unusual lights on the same stretch of road traveled by the Cash-Landrum party.

- Roughneck Jerry McDonald, twenty-four, watched the sky from his Dayton home. "I heard a sound like a rumble, and I thought it was the Goodyear blimp," he said. "It was kind of triangular or diamond-shaped and had two twin torches that were shooting brilliant blue flames out the back."

- Fifty-five-year-old bakery clerk Bell Magee saw lights from her home in nearby Eastgate. "It was bright, like the lights of a football field, but up in the sky," the *Chronicle* quoted her as saying.

- Off-duty Dayton police officer L.L. Walker recalled seeing several helicopters in the area sometime in late December.

- Jon Mark McDonald, who later became a Lake Jackson police officer, reported seeing a similar object about two years later near Cleveland. "Everybody was riding me about it—thought I was crazy," McDonald told the *Chronicle*. "But I just knew it wasn't an airplane, because I've been working in the U.S. Army Reserves and know about every fixed-wing (craft) there is."

Petitioning the Government

Determined to find out what they had seen, and what had caused their illnesses, Mrs. Landrum began calling Washington.

One person she reached referred her to the Arial Phenomena Research Organization (APRO). A UFO researcher with the group, Alan Hendry, suggested she write her congressmen.

U.S. Representative Charles Wilson, now famous for the Oscar-nominated film dramatizing his involvement in building support for CIA operations in Afghanistan, sent Mrs. Landrum a form letter explaining that the government had stopped investigating UFO incidents years earlier. The letter listed a number of private organizations like APRO that might be able to help her. "I turned it over and wrote him a letter back....and I told him exactly how I felt," she said.

U.S. Senator Lloyd Bentsen responded with a personal letter, suggesting that Mrs. Landrum travel to Austin and meet with the judge advocate at Bergstrom.

The transcript from that meeting reflects initial confusion among all present about why the meeting was taking place.

"Is there anything in particular you hope to gain by coming and talking with um...to people in the Air Force?" Captain Camp asked near the end of the meeting, after the officers had politely interviewed the trio about their experience.

The Air Force officers seemed to take a we're-from-the-government, we're-here-to-help, but-we-really-can't-do-anything stance. Camp explained that as Representative Wilson's letter pointed out, the government's Project Blue Book had indeed been closed since 1969. After more than twenty years of cataloguing UFO sightings, the Air Force saw little point in continuing.

Some might argue that the government's decision to officially get out of the UFO business also gave it a degree of plausible deniability. With no mandate to investigate strange sightings, authorities may have felt less compelled to truthfully and publicly explain strange things seen in the sky. Meanwhile, the Cold War continued. The public's fear of nuclear annihilation, although less acute, remained pervasive. And though a few spots in the Communist permafrost may have begun to thaw a bit by the early 1980s, ufologists contend the government still had plenty of secret operations to hide.

A plethora of private organizations stepped into fill the void when the government stopped officially investigating

UFOs. While these ranged from the skeptical to the evangelical, several took the objective, scientific study of the phenomena quite seriously. Without official government sanction, they lacked—or in the eyes of some gained—a degree of credibility.

"There's a lot of quacks out there, there really is, that's supposed to be big UFO dealers and wheelers," Mrs. Landrum said at Bergstrom. "They're not after hunting the truth, they're after something...proving something that's unreal... What was up there was real. It hurt us. It wasn't from outer space, either."

"And they're out for a story," Cash chimed in.

"Well, sometimes they're out to make a sensational story," Mrs. Landrum agreed. "They'll get people to buy their publication."

Captain Camp, meanwhile, still couldn't understand why Senator Bentsen suggested the ladies drive to Austin. "We're an agency that has not investigated UFOs in almost eleven years," he explained.

"Well, he didn't tell me to come here for you to investigate UFOs, he said to come here to file a claim," Cash said.

With the goal of the meeting finally clear, Captain Camp quickly made arrangements to have the appropriate paperwork mailed to Mrs. Landrum in Dayton. He stressed, however, that he could not provide legal advice and suggested the women contact a private attorney if they felt they needed legal representation.

The women did just that.

Attorney Peter Gersten took up the case. Then the executive director of Citizens Against UOF Secrecy, Gersten had filed Freedom of Information Act lawsuits against several government agencies seeking records related to unexplained sightings. After the Air Force denied the trio's claim for compensation, Gersten filed a federal lawsuit seeking $20 million in damages. The case marked what is believed to be the first time UFO witnesses sued the government.

A federal judge dismissed the case in 1986, finding that government agencies did not own or operate any aircraft like the one seen near Huffman in 1980. A few years later, attorney Clay Ford of Gulf Breeze, Florida, told the *Chronicle* he would try to have the case reopened on procedural grounds. He also pressed on with an unsuccessful attempt to negotiate a movie deal for his clients.

The same *Chronicle* article reported that after an *Unsolved Mysteries* broadcast of the Cash-Landrum story in February 1991, a couple of callers to program's hotline speculated that the trio may have encountered an experimental aircraft powered by nuclear energy. In his book about the case, Schuessler cites a sketchy, third-hand account of an experimental aircraft being flown from Albuquerque to Houston's Ellington Field on the night in question. Schuessler also dramatizes an unproven "likely scenario" involving a secret military unit training for a second attempt to rescue the American hostages being held in Iran. Government sources denied all such rumors.

The two women ultimately received no government compensation for their injuries and claimed their illnesses left them unable to work. Cash battled three rounds of cancer but lived until 1998, dying on the 18th anniversary of that ill-fated bingo trip.

In later years, Mrs. Landrum seemed to regret breaking her vow of silence about the strange craft she saw over the tall pines. She told the *Chronicle* that fellow Daytonites called her "the UFO lady," and that other children teased her grandson.

"To put it point blank, what we thought maybe you could give us an answer of where to go from here, or what to do, because I'm gonna find the answer," she had vowed to the Air Force officers in Austin. "It might take me a lifetime, but I intend to find it."

According to records on file with the Montgomery County Clerk's office, Mrs. Landrum died September 12, 2007. Her obituary in the *Big Thicket Messenger* stated, "Vickie liked to play bingo, computer games and sew, but above all she loved to play with and take care of her grandchildren." She left behind five children, fourteen grandchildren, and two dozen great-grandchildren. But if she ever found the answers she sought about what she saw that night on Farm Road 1485, she took them with her.

Chapter 15:
UFO Lore Crashes and Burns
on the Border

The folklore of UFOs and of the Texas/Mexico border share some common themes. From flying saucers and border bandits arise murky tales and fantastic legends. The truth can be as elusive as a South Texas *bruja* soaring through the night. As is the case with those mythical, transfiguring witches, UFO stories live more in whispered rumor than in the memories of eyewitnesses.

Texas' more tenuous UFO tales include a pair about alleged saucer crashes along that stretch of the Rio Grande that descends from the Big Bend toward the Gulf. These stories illustrate not only the difficulty in separating fact from fiction where two nations meet, but the fractious and sometimes virulent nature of ufology in the 1980s.

Little Burned Men
A decade after the Air Force shut Project Blue Book, no government agency officially or consistently investigated, catalogued, or debunked UFO sightings. This left the issue wide open to all kinds of speculation. Fewer Texans may have witnessed UFOs in the '70s and '80s than in the preceding three decades, but no one can say for sure since no one kept official records. Widespread UFO flaps no longer captured the public imagination, but some individual witnesses' tales grew

more sinister and complex. Stories circulated about close encounters and abductions by mind-controlling aliens.

A number of private groups took on the task of investigating UFO reports. True believers aligned themselves with some of these organizations, staunch skeptics with others. Sometimes, their feuds went public and got ugly.

A few ufologists uncovered compelling evidence that some government employees kept up Cold War secrecy and intentional misinformation well into the 1970s. This provided rich fodder for the paranoia prone and gave rise to tales about malevolent aliens that mutilated cattle, impregnated women, manufactured cocaine, and shot people with beams that caused acid reflux. This environment spawned a spate of UFO stories that brought unusual lights in the sky down to earth. Tales began to emerge about spaceship crashes and alien corpses. Commonly, "evidence" of a flying saucer crash arrived anonymously in the mailbox of someone who stood to gain financially from such a revelation.

Perhaps some unwitting ufologists picked up copies of Frank Scully's 1950 tome, *Behind the Flying Saucers*, at garage sales without knowing his sources had been discredited as con men shortly after its publication. Maybe Roswell UFO champion Jesse Marcel's claims of unearthly wreckage in the New Mexico desert inspired Southwestern imaginations. Or perhaps some believed so strongly in visitors from outer space that their beliefs could not be shaken by a lack of hard evidence. For whatever reason, the ambiguity of the Mexican side of the border proved fertile ground for rumors about crashed flying saucers and their unfortunate and unearthly occupants.

Photos from Laredo

Several UFO Web sites today offer this sparse, copied-and-pasted description of the better known of two Texas border incidents:

201

> August 1948—Laredo, Texas
> Four officers witnessed the crash of an object and the recovery of bodies 38 miles south of Laredo, Texas in Mexico. The information came from an NBC affiliate in Chicago, who received it from Army security.

The longer version of the story begins in Maryland, where Willard McIntyre founded the Mutual Anomaly Research Center and Evaluation Network (MARCEN). McIntyre claimed he began receiving letters from a mysterious Tennesssean shortly after publishing the inaugural issue of MARCEN's journal in 1978. The source claimed to be a former Navy photographer stationed at White Sands Missile Base in New Mexico. This military shutterbug said he snapped shots of test sites following atomic bomb blasts.

The source—anonymous to all but McIntyre—gave a very detailed account of the events of July 7 and 8, 1948. At 1:22 p.m., the Distant Early Warning (DEW) system supposedly picked up an object on radar over Washington State headed southeast at more than two thousand miles per hour. Two fighter pilots scrambled from "Dias Air Base" in Texas to intercept the object over Albuquerque. Like Bugs Bunny, the UFO apparently found Albuquerque a good place to make a left turn. As the F-94 jets neared, the object angled ninety degrees toward "East Texas." Other pilots then noticed the object slowing and wobbling before it disappeared from radar. All of this supposedly happened in just over an hour's time.

Although the object's last known trajectory put it on track for Arkansas, "expert triangulation" somehow fixed the point of the object's demise at thirty miles south of Laredo. Author William Steinman, in his privately published book *UFO Crash at Aztec*, contends that Secretary of State George Marshall himself intervened with Mexican authorities to get permission for U.S. military personnel to cross the border and retrieve the wreckage, claiming it was a malfunctioned rocket or test craft. Air Force and Army units arrived at the site sometime after 6:30 p.m.

This is where the mysterious photographer inserts himself into the story. The scene commander called Washington and requested a photographic team. McIntyre's anonymous source said he and others left New Mexico in an Army L-19 Bird Dog at 9:30 p.m. and arrived in Mexico three hours and forty-five minutes later to find a disc-shaped aircraft crashed into a hillside.

When the plane reached the crash site, it circled the smoldering saucer and landed on a makeshift runway, according to the anonymous source. Soldiers waited for the disc to cool down and then moved a four-foot, six-inch body away from the wreckage.

Several Web sites and '90s-vintage UFO books describe the ear-, nose-, and lipless traveler as having a very large head, long arms, and claws. Military doctors—who apparently preferred to conduct an on-scene autopsy instead of first moving the body to a nice, clean laboratory somewhere—reportedly found no reproductive organs or muscle fiber in the torso. The being's bone structure also appeared more complicated than a human's. For some reason, UFO authors seem consistently compelled to describe the crashed pilot's skin as having "the texture of a human female breast." The military loaded the unfortunate flyer's body into a C-47 and left the scene not quite twenty-four hours after the crash.

As for the mysterious aircraft, McIntyre's source said it appeared to be made of "earthly" materials, although the exterior hull's metal proved so hard it could only be cut using diamond-edged tools. Ufologists perpetuating crash stories in the 1980s often referred to "honeycombed" alloys, and the

Laredo case is no exception. Also, a strong foil material supposedly littered the area, but the military made sure every scrap was confiscated before leaving. Steinman, who cites several other sketchy, third-hand recollections in addition to the McIntyre letters, described the craft as measuring about ninety feet across and twenty-five feet thick at the center, tapering to about five feet at the edges. The photographer last saw the wreckage loaded onto trucks headed northwest.

Back in New Mexico, the photographic team spent the next three weeks developing more than five hundred negatives under the watchful eye of armed guards, who took all the prints to Washington. The source claimed that several years later, he secretly borrowed the negatives, duplicated forty of them, and replaced the originals.

The photographer, who feared prosecution if he revealed himself, sent two eight-by-ten pictures and their negatives to McIntyre as the two exchanged correspondence in 1978-79. Although McIntyre first believed the crashed vehicle to be a light plane of some type, he eventually bought into the flying saucer story, noting that the source's credentials "checked out."

Another common element this tales shares with many other UFO stories is McIntyre's contention that he sent the negatives to experts at Eastman Kodak, who analyzed them and found no evidence of "deliberate" hoaxing.

Steinman's book claims that MARCEN released the photos to the press on August 22, 1980, prompting a media frenzy that lasted several weeks. However, a search of a database containing historic archives from more than three hundred newspapers turned up no saucer-crash stories in late August 1980.

The more skeptical UFO researchers had a field day with McIntyre's second-hand tale. One group, Ground Saucer Watch, performed some sort of computer analysis on the photos and came to the conclusion that the unlucky flyer was likely a laboratory monkey. Other groups dismissed that idea but found many discrepancies in the story.

Ron Schaffner, former investigations director of the Ohio UFO Investigators League (OUFOIL), used the story to teach newby ufologists about common investigatory pitfalls. Some of OUFOIL's members believed McIntyre, but most did not, and OUFOIL's name became erroneously linked to the Laredo investigation. The organization initiated its own investigation after McIntyre refused to share his documentation with its members.

OUFOIL's findings include the following highlights:

- Eastman Kodak could not provide documentation related to its examination of the negatives, and its spokesman said that the company would not perform such analysis.
- The burn unit chief of staff at the Shriner's Hospital for Crippled Children in Cincinnati said head swelling is a common side effect of human incineration.
- The DEW radar racking system, set up to provide warning of enemy air attacks, did not become operational until 1957.
- Abilene's Dyess (not "Dias") Air Force Base did not open until 1956.
- F-94 fighter jets did not fly until 1949, and L-19 Bird Dogs did not take to the sky until 1954. The latter craft, a light recognizance plane, held no more than two people and no cargo.
- OUFOIL members spotted what appeared to be terrestrial cabling and eyeglass frames in the photographs.
- Quite obviously, another ninety-degree turn would have been required to put the crashed craft south of the Rio Grande instead of north of the Red River.

"The ... incident could not have happened with the information given," Schaffner concluded.

The Majestic Twelve

As with the Aztec hoax three decades earlier, Hollywood plays a supporting role in the second and sketchier border crash story. And as with the Laredo tale, the evidence arrived anonymously, this time carrying an Albuquerque postmark.

Television producer Jaime Shandera shared much in common with 1940s *Variety* writer Frank Scully; both men had their ears bent by someone with a vested interest in alleged New Mexican flying saucer crashes. In Shandera's case, Roswell researcher William L. Moore told his Hollywood contact that a small group of U.S. Air Force officials wanted to tell the world that the military had been harboring and colluding with space aliens for years.

Shandera checked his home mailbox on December 11, 1984, to find a heavily sealed package containing an undeveloped role of 35mm film. The developed images showed two top-secret documents: a September 24, 1947, executive order signed by Harry S. Truman that purportedly created "Operation Majestic Twelve," and a briefing document dated November 18, 1952, that updated president-elect Dwight D. Eisenhower on the status and membership of this elite group of policymakers in charge of intergalactic relations. Timothy Good, a British ufologist, apparently received a similar package. Both released their revelations to the press in 1987.

Once the documents became public, experts at the National Archives quickly dismissed them as frauds. Fonts, formats, date references, paper size, and signatures did not jive with historical records. Some ufologists surmised Moore might have created the fake memos. Others suspected the involvement of an Air Force sergeant who fed outlandish and elaborate misinformation to Moore and to an electronics specialist who serendipitously picked up secret signals emanating from Albuquerque's Kirtland Air Force Base.

This particularly bizarre chapter of UFO history bolsters the arguments of those who believe the phenomenon can be largely attributed to the ill-advised actions of government agencies, or at least to rogue government employees. Ufologist Peter Brookesmith strongly hints in his book *UFO: The Government Files*, that the so-called MJ-12 hoax may have grown from misinformation planted by U.S. Air Force Office of Special Investigations (AFOSI) Sergeant Richard L. Doty.

Doty began feeding outlandish tales in late 1980 to an Albuquerque ufologist named Paul Bennewitz. Earlier that year, Bennewitz witnessed the hypnotic regression of a woman who believed herself to be the victim of alien abduction. He became convinced that aliens implanted a device in her head to control her actions. An electronics expert, Bennewitz set out to prove his theory by monitoring radio signals.

Unfortunately for Bennewitz, he did pick up mysterious signals and believed them to be alien communication. In reality, the signals emanated from secret experiments at Kirtland. Bennewitz approached the Air Force with his "evidence" and gained an audience with Doty. Curiously, the AFOSI chose not to simply refute Bennewitz's alien theories and send him on his way. Since Bennewitz insisted on continuing his unofficial radio surveillance, someone at Kirtland decided to supply him with misinformation so outlandish that no one would believe him if he ever "leaked" it.

Not long before Doty's meeting with Bennewitz, an AFOSI representative asked Moore to spy on the electrician. Moore agreed because he thought doing so would help him get to the "truth" about the government's involvement with aliens. AFOSI continued misleading both men until Bennewitz had a nervous breakdown in 1985. Several months later, AFOSI gave Doty the boot after discovering unrelated fabrications.

Brookesmith and other more skeptical ufologists connected dots between Doty, Moore, and the MJ-12 papers. But despite immediate debunking after their release, true believers picked them up and ran with them. Among these were conspiracy theorist Steinman, who also believed the criminal convictions against Scully's Aztec sources resulted from charges trumped up by MJ-12 operatives.

Other people later came forward with additional "government documents" mentioning MJ-12. One writer posted on the fledgling Internet claims that aliens had left behind a hostage on Earth named KRLL. The ufologist also asserted that MJ-12 ran the international drug trade and assassinated President Kennedy.

Bogeys and Brush

The supposed MJ-12 Eisenhower briefing described the recovery of alien bodies in Roswell in 1947 and on the Mexican border on December 6, 1950. That date deserves a footnote in history. At least three bona fide accounts—one from President Truman's own memoirs—refer to a national security alert that morning.

The Cold War with the Russians and the very hot war in Korea had the whole world on edge that December. Even President Truman sincerely believed that World War III might be at hand.

British Prime Minister Clement Attlee had crossed the pond a couple of days earlier. In a November 30 press conference, Truman said in response to a reporter's question that the United States would consider using all weapons at its disposal to deal with the North Koreans. Concerned that America might drop another atomic bomb, Attlee hightailed it to Washington.

Just before a meeting with Attlee on the morning of December 6, Truman's staff told him of northern radar installations picking up large formations of planes approaching the United States. Various White House and newspaper accounts from the time differ on whether the signals originated in Alaska or Maine and on whether they were ultimately attributed to atmospheric conditions, flocks of geese, or misidentified aircraft. Whatever its origin or cause, the false alarm only lasted about an hour.

The MJ-12 papers, however, link this brief national security alert to another flying saucer crash along the U.S.-Mexican border. Few details survive, apart from a grammatically challenged statement in the alleged briefing to Eisenhower. This paragraph followed a description of the Roswell incident:

On 06 December 1950, a second object, probably of similar origin, impacted the earth at high speed in the El Indio Guerrero area of the Texas Mexico border after following a long trajectory through the atmosphere. By the time a search team arrived, what remained of the object had been almost totally incinerated. Such material as could be recovered was transported to the AEC [Atomic Energy Commission] facility in Sandia, New Mexico, for further study.

With only this sketchy description to go on, Dennis Stacy and other members of the Mutual UFO Network (MUFON) made three trips to Mexico in the 1990s in attempts to find the crash site. They talked to old timers on both sides of the border near El Indio, Texas, and Guerrero, Mexico, which flank the Rio Grande southeast of Eagle Pass and Piedras Negras. One life-long Guerrero resident, Rosendo Flores, recalled a fireball crashing and starting a grass fire on El Rancho del Griegos, or the Ranch of the Greeks. The military arrived from Piedras Negras a couple of days later to haul off some mysterious cargo.

The MUFON researchers ultimately tracked down the ranch's then-owners and learned of a mysterious hole that appeared on that ranch within the timeframe the supposed flying saucer incident occurred. One area resident recalled a tractor falling into the hole. More than a dozen locals pitched in during an unsuccessful attempt to find the crash site.

On their final trip in 1994, Stacey's team enjoyed better directions from the ranch foreman and located a small but inconclusive depression. John Yates, a salesman for the Psychological Corporation in Fort Worth, came along on this outing and brought a metal detector. He didn't even find bottle caps.

The researchers believe they finally found their answer in a book on military aviation history. *Wings Over the Mexican Border: Pioneer Military Aviation History in the Big Bend* chronicled the January 1944 crash of a military plane about seven miles from Guerrero.

Reconnaissance planes began flying on the American side of the border in the 1920s. The borderlands aviation book, written by historian Kenneth Baxter Ragsdale, highlights an airstrip on the Elmo Johnson ranch. Johnson volunteered his land in the Big Bend area after fugitive Mexican revolutionaries crossed the Rio Grande and attempted to steal his livestock in 1929. The emergency landing strip on Johnson's ranch supported airfields in El Paso, Del Rio, Laredo, and Marfa. For some fourteen years, pilots low on fuel, threatened by inclement weather, or in need of a hot meal and a warm bed would drop in on the Johnson place.

Military pilots patrolled the Rio Grande throughout the 1930s, but as World War II loomed, their presence was needed elsewhere. In July 1942, the commander of the Southern Defense Command requested that the Civil Air Patrol keep an eye on the Mexican border. Major Harry K. Coffey of Portland, Oregon, took on this responsibility. As a result, many volunteer pilots brought their own planes from the Pacific Northwest to help secure the nation's southern border during wartime. Based in El Paso, the Southern Liaison Patrol (SLP) flew two round trips daily on irregular schedules to Del Rio and two to Douglas, Arizona.

Over the next two years, the SLP would make more than six thousand flights along the border, usually with substandard equipment and sometimes in dangerously inclement weather. The flyers took it upon themselves to gather as much intelligence as possible about airfields in Mexico rumored to be under Axis control. One news report from the El Paso *Herald-Post* reported the capture of six Japanese nationals, a German, and an Italian operating airfields in Chihuahua, according to Ragsdale.

Occasionally, the zealous and resourceful SLP pilots ventured farther south than international treaties probably allowed, but U.S. authorities found their work quite useful. The information they provided enabled significant military troop reductions in the region, as well as the prompt apprehension of suspicious characters crossing the Rio Grande.

Despite the dangers it faced, the SLP lost only two pilots in the nearly two years it patrolled the border. Their deaths, however, remain shrouded in mystery. Three days after the accident that took their lives, a public information officer at Fort McIntosh in Laredo issued a statement on January 19, 1944, reporting that lieutenants Bayard Henderson and Harry Hewitt died when their plane "crashed and burned" while "on routine patrol twenty miles from Eagle Pass."

Retired officers interviewed by Ragsdale in 1984 recalled that the incident had been "hushed up" and was rumored to have been the result of a "gunnery school accident." In fact, the Army Air Force conducted advanced training at the Eagle Pass Army Airfield at the time. Over a gunnery range near El Indio, student pilots fired lived rounds at targets towed by other aircraft.

211

But an explanation as plausible as friendly fire was never verified by the military. And Lieutenant Hewitt's vague death certificate adds another layer of uncertainty. The Del Rio mortuary that issued it failed to list a cause of death. Because of this, it took two and a half years and a literal act of Congress for his widow to receive survivor's benefits.

Unsolved Mysteries, Unproven Theories
Another mention of the December 1950 crash comes from ufologist Kevin Randle, who wrote an entire book about the MJ-12 documents. Randle and a few other ufologists referred to the crash's location as "near Del Rio," a larger city seventy miles upstream on the Rio Grande. Linking the incident to the MJ-12 papers, however, makes it obvious Randle is referring to the Guerrero crash.

Inconsistencies regarding the Texas UFO tale mentioned in the papers fueled Randle's own skepticism about the documents' authenticity. He heard and attempted to verify a third-hand story from Iowa writer Warren Smith, who claimed the crash happened while an acquaintance's wife vacationed on a Big Bend dude ranch. The woman supposedly wrote her husband several letters detailing strange behavior by military personnel and men in black suits. However, Randle eventually came to believe that Smith made up the story, possibly with the intention of "discovering" the letters and making them public.

Although thoroughly debunked by some, this pair of borderlands UFO legends for others remains in the realm of the chupacabra, the Seven Cities of Cibolo, and Alsate's ghost— stories too good to be ruined by the truth, whatever that may be.

Chapter 16:
A Cow Country Classic:
Bovina 1995

Texans have a saying about air travel: You can go to hell, but you will have a layover in Dallas. This is particularly true when flying American or Southwest, since both airlines call North Texas home.

May 25, 1995, proved to be a long and eventful Labor Day for the crew of America West Flight 564. After departing from Tampa, Florida, they made their obligatory stop at Dallas/Fort Worth International Airport, then continued toward their final destination—Las Vegas, Nevada. The weather did them no favors. As they crossed the Texas Panhandle and neared the state line, thunderclouds flashed and rumbled to the north.

The lead flight attendant secured himself in the cockpit and gazed out the windows, while the pilot and copilot monitored instruments and radio traffic. The attendant was the first to notice lights in the sky that had nothing to with the thunderstorm. A horizontal row of bright, blue-white strobes flashed in a left-to-right sequence to the north of the Boeing 757 and at a lower altitude.

The flight attendant called the lights to the attention of co-pilot John J. Waller, and Captain Eugene Tollefson left his seat to get a look. He spotted the lights just in time to see a lightning flash silhouette their source in the night sky—a classic cigar-shaped UFO. The crew estimated its altitude at 30,000 to 35,000 feet and its length at 300 to 400 feet.

The time of the sighting varies among retold accounts. Some confusion could be expected since the Texas-New Mexico state line serves as the divider between the Mountain and Central time zones in that region. Perhaps the most authoritative source, Walter N. Webb, thoroughly investigated the case on behalf of the UFO Research Coalition, a joint venture of the Center for UFO Studies (CUFOS), the Fund for UFO Research, and the Mutual UFO Network. Webb's final report on the sighting pegs the time at 10:25 p.m. Mountain Daylight Time (or 11:35 p.m. by Texas clocks).

Webb obtained tape recordings of relevant radio traffic from that night after filing a Freedom of Information Act (FOI) request with the Federal Aviation Administration (FAA). Transcripts of the tapes, as published in Webb's final report on the case, reveal that co-pilot Waller created quite a stir among the staff at the Albuquerque Air Route Traffic Control Center when he radioed and asked them to check their radar:

Flight 564: Center, Cactus 564

Air traffic controller (ATC) 1: Cactus 564, go ahead.

Flight 564: Yeah, off to our three o'clock, we got some strobes out there. Can you tell us what it is?

ATC 1: Uh, I'll tell you what. That's some, uh, right now I don't know what it is right now. There's a restricted area that's used by the military out there in the daytime.

Flight 564: Yeah, it's pretty odd.

...

Flight 564: 564, did you paint that object at all on your radar?

ATC 1: Cactus 564, no I don't and talking to three or four guys around here, no one knows what that is. Never heard about that.

Flight 564: So nobody's painting it at all?

ATC 1: Cactus 564, say again?

Flight 564: There's nothing on the radars on the other centers at all on that particular area, that object that's up in the air?

ATC 1: Uh, it's up in the air?

Flight 564: A-ffirmative!

ATC 1: No! No one knows anything about it. What's the altitude about?

Flight 564: I don't know. Probably right around 30,000 or so. And it's, uh, there's a strobe. It starts from going counterclockwise, and the length is unbelievable.

Over the next hour, the excited air traffic controllers contacted Cannon Air Force Base in nearby Clovis, New Mexico, and the North American Aerospace Defense Command (NORAD). They also discussed the sighting with a couple of American Airlines pilots and a Southwest Airlines crew flying in the area, but none of them spotted what Flight 564 witnessed. A military flyer apparently saw a craft at about the same altitude, but none of the investigative reports describe it as a UFO.

The tape transcripts also show geographic confusion and spacecraft-leaning assumptions on the part of the air traffic controllers. For example, the controller who initially spoke to Waller incorrectly told personnel at Cannon that the UFO had been spotted above TAIBAN, the code for Cannon's Military Operation Area (MOA).

ATC 1: Guy at 39,000 says he sees something at 30,000. The length is unbelievable, and it has a strobe on it.

Cannon: Uh-huh.

ATC 1: This is not good.

Cannon: What does that mean?

ATC 1: I don't know. It's a UFO or something. It's that Roswell crap again.

Cannon: Where's it at now?

ATC 1: He says it's right in TAIBAN.

Cannon: It's right in TAIBAN? No, we haven't seen nothing like that.

ATC 1: OK. Keep your eyes open.

A second air traffic controller told the military pilot to look for the UFO on his right as he flew east toward Texas, then corrected himself and told the flyer to look out his left window. And a third controller later told NORAD the sighting had occurred near Tucumcari, New Mexico.

ATC 3: …We've tried everybody else and nobody else's—this guy definitely saw it run all the way down the side of the airplane. Said it was a pretty interesting thing out there.

NORAD: OK, it was at 30,000 feet?

ATC 3: 30,000 feet.

NORAD: It was like long and…

ATC 3: Yeah, it's right out of the "The X-Files." I mean, it's a definite UFO or something like that. I mean…

NORAD: And it's, oh, y'all are serious about this.

ATC 3: Yeah, he's real serious about it, too, and he looked at it and saw it. No balloons were reported tonight, nothing in the area.

...

NORAD: How long did he think it was?

ATC 3: He said it was 300 to 400 foot long.

NORAD: Holy…smokes!

ATC 3: Yeah, and we don't have any air carriers out there so, that are strobing along.

NORAD: Well [unintelligible] I wonder if any of our aerostats got loose or something, because we don't have any aerostats out there.

ATC 3: Yeah, not that far to the north.

NORAD: I mean, it really would sound like an aerostat, but I don't think ours are that big though.

ATC 3: Yeah, no. They're more like a blimp rather than—this sounded like some sort of a flying hot dog or something.

Plotting points of interest based Flight 564's path and interviews with Waller, Webb estimated that the plane and the UFO were both on the Texas side of the state line when the incident occurred. As the plane passed south of Bovina, a small Parmer County community not far from Clovis, the UFO hovered somewhere north of nearby Friona, backlit by a thunderstorm rumbling even farther north across Deaf Smith County. And despite its proximity to Cannon, Webb found that this mid-northern Panhandle region did not fall within that base's MOA. Instead, these rural communities underlie Air Refueling Anchor (AR) 623 used by flyers from Dyess Air Force Base in Abilene, Texas.

The XIT Files

In spite of its table-flat terrain and semiarid climate, the transstate region where Flight 564 spotted its UFO is thickly dotted with towns whose names describe the basis for the local economy. A Sunday driver touring the area might pass through Hereford, Lariat, or Muleshoe on the Texas side, or perhaps Ranchvale in New Mexico. Adapting to this cowfolk's paradise can be a bit tough for the Air Force families stationed at Cannon who fail to cultivate an appreciation for feedlots, grain silos, and chicken-fried steak.

Bovina, the presumed focal point of the Flight 564 sighting, sits along U.S. Highway 60. That road forms the short side of a triangle with corners where Interstate 27 meets it in Canyon to the north and meets U.S. Highway 84 in Lubbock to the south. Highways 60 and 84 converge several miles southwest of Bovina at Farwell and then run together due west through the New Mexican towns of Texico and Clovis.

The community that became Bovina originated after Charles B. and John V. Farwell promised to build the $3-million Texas State Capitol in exchange for 3 million acres of land in the Panhandle. The resulting XIT Ranch, which covered a vast expanse across the Texas high plains, soon established the Hay Hook Line Camp in Parmer County. In 1898, the Pecos and Northern Texas Railway laid tracks across the ranch and placed a switch at the camp. Cowboys then commonly fed cottonseed to cattle, and they unloaded shipments of it at the switch. Cattle began gathering around the tracks to forage for spilled seeds and often relaxed to chew their cud. Annoyed rail men, who had to stop their trains to shoo the animals away, dubbed the spot Bull Town. More gentile residents of the area changed the name to Bovina when the post office opened in 1899. The community boomed around the turn of the century and for a time became the world's largest-volume shipping point for cattle. Although Bovina's population never topped 2,000, U.S. Census records show that it grew steadily throughout the 20th Century.

Unfettered by urban sprawl, the Texas Panhandle remains the kind of place where sky watchers enjoy unobstructed views, where cold, dry air produces sundogs in winter, and where starlight gets little competition from city lights. It's also a place where scientists and military personnel can send things up in the sky without bothering too many people very often.

What It Wasn't

Webb checked out several possibilities in his quest to discover the source of the long, wingless mystery craft that the Flight 564 crew reported seeing that late-spring night.

Cannon, the air force base nearest the sighting, would seem the most likely source for the unidentified object. The 27th Fighter Wing moved to Cannon in 1959, and that unit has been involved in every significant military skirmish since Korea. In the mid-1990s, its air fleet included a couple of

1970s-era electronic warfare planes not found elsewhere in the country. However, Webb's report indicates that the Albuquerque air traffic controllers checked with Cannon and another unspecified air base in the vicinity and found no evidence of military activity the night in question.

Webb confirmed that Captain Tollefson also saw two B-1 bombers flying at 35,000 feet that night, but their size, lighting patterns, and altitude did not match the UFO's. Therefore, Webb focused on three possibilities: an aerostat surveillance balloon, a night advertising aircraft or blimp, or an aerial refueling operation.

The investigator quickly ruled out the advertising craft hypothesis, although such aerial contraptions can look odd and are not uncommonly mistaken for UFOs. Lighted advertising planes fly low so that people on the ground can read their messages. Such a craft would not climb as high as 30,000 feet, and the airline crew would not have seen its unusual lights from above.

Next, Webb looked into the aerostat angle. These large balloons help defend the Texas-Mexican border against drug runners, but the nearest floated some three hundred miles south of Bovina in May 1995. At 233 feet long, aerostats approach the length of the UFO described by the crew aboard Flight 564, but their tethers only reach about 15,000 feet, and their three lights flash in unison, not in sequence.

Webb also contacted Dyess in Abilene. Again, he doubted the pilots and flight attendant would have confused a 134-foot, bottom-lit KC-135 or KC-10 refueling plane for a UFO. The base's flight plans did include scheduled trips into AR 623 that day by two B-1B bombers, but even if the fighter jets had rendezvoused with a refueling craft, they should have been back in Abilene hours before the sighting. But Tollefson's report may prove the Dyess pilots ran a bit late that evening.

The sources contacted by the air traffic controllers reported no weather balloons aloft that night, but the FAA tapes reveal no mention of much larger and stranger-looking scientific balloons. Webb did not indicate in his final report whether he contacted anyone in Fort Sumner, about sixty miles west of Clovis. The National Scientific Balloon Facility (now the Columbia Scientific Balloon Facility) took over an old Army airfield there in 1987. (See Chapter 10.)

Danny Ball, site manager for the facility's home base in Palestine, Texas, fully expected the Bovina object to be a Fort Sumner balloon, since May is the height of New Mexico's launch season. After checking records, however, he found that scientists sent balloons aloft in April and June of 1995, but not in May.

On the Small Screen

The Bovina sighting might not have made a blip on the ufology radar if not for those air traffic controllers back in Albuquerque. According to Webb's report, two of them contacted the syndicated television show "Sightings" a couple of months after the incident. The television program's producers followed Webb's lead in filing an FOI request and included bits of audio from the FAA tapes in the November 4, 1995, episode.

Webb identifies the "Sightings" tipsters as air traffic controllers as Steven Jones, who also contacted CUFOS, and Steven Kubala, but adds underlined and in parentheses, "Both individuals' names remain strictly confidential." Why he then included them in a report available for purchase by the public remains unclear. (Webb also refers to the pilot and co-pilot by name, and notes that they were none too happy about the "Sightings" broadcast. He was unable to track down the lead flight attendant, who left the airline and moved to another state after the sighting.)

Perhaps Kubala, as is often the case with those who cry UFO, later regretted the notoriety.

"In the beginning the controller proved very cooperative, allowing two long telephone interviews (totaling more than one and a half hours)," Webb wrote in his 1996 final report. "But since then he as refused to return my telephone messages or reply to my letters."

Webb eventually became skeptical of Kubala after realizing that his account of the events of May 25, 1995, did not completely jibe with those of the actual witnesses. "In retrospect, Kubala's version of the UFO event seemed to me somewhat imaginative and certain aspects later proved untrue," Webb wrote.

For example, Kubala claimed that after Flight 564 landed in Las Vegas, nine passengers told the crew they had also seen the object. But Waller and Tollefson both denied speaking to passenger witnesses.

Also, the last section of the FAA tapes chronicles an exchange between Albuquerque and NORAD involving an object spotted on radar about three counties north of Bovina. NORAD eventually picked up a transponder code that identified the object as a run-of-the-mill aircraft. Kubala later said he followed up with NORAD the next morning and was told that radar picked up another target over the Panhandle about an hour after the airline sighting. The controller claimed he had been told the object repeatedly accelerated from zero to 1,000 miles per hour. However, given his growing skepticism of the source and the fact that NORAD provided no record of the follow-up call, Webb ultimately discounted Kubala's claim.

Regardless of the air traffic controllers' possible embellishments, the FAA tapes—along with statements and drawings provided by the pilot and co-pilot—clearly prove that the crew of Flight 564 saw something they did not understand as Labor Day weekend drew to a close in 1995.

Flight 564: Albuquerque, when you get a chance? Cactus 564.

ATC 2: Yes, sir. Go ahead.

Flight 564: We're all huddled up here talking about it. [With the] lightning, you could see the dark object. It was like a cigar shape from the altitude we could see it. The length is what sort of got us a little confused because it looked like it was three- to four-hundred feet long. I don't know if it's a wire with strobes on it. The strobe started going left to right counterclockwise. It was a pretty eerie sight. But it had some strobes on it going left to right.

ACT 2: Don't mean to be funny, but I do believe I saw that in a movie once, didn't I?

Flight 564: Well, three of us up here saw it.

CHAPTER 17:
THE STEPHENVILLE LIGHTS:
"WE ALL FLIPPED OUT."

When Sarah Cannady bought a long-established used and rare bookstore in downtown Stephenville called The Literary Lion, she made her advertising slogan "the bookstore time forgot."

As 2008 began, she decided late one night to do some rearranging in her two-story shop, located a couple of blocks from the Erath County courthouse in an old dry goods store built in 1904. Among other things, she moved her collection of books on ufology and science fiction to a shelf closer to her establishment's front door, one of the more visible display areas.

Not long after that, Cannady began to notice an upturn in sales of those books, particularly titles dealing with UFOs. Thinking her "greedy capitalist scheme" (as she later called it) seemed to be working, she gleefully continued to ring up sales of UFO books that had been sitting unmolested on their previous shelf for months.

Preoccupied with getting the new year off to a robust financial start, Cannady readily admits she had not been paying much attention to local news. One day that January, a customer asked her what she thought about the wave of UFO sightings going on in and around her home town, a university community of 15,000 located sixty-six miles southwest of Fort Worth. "What UFOs?" she asked.

Sarah Cannady outside her bookstore

"I live like a monk here," she laughed in recalling how she first became aware of the sightings that had been occurring right under her literary nose. "Turns out the whole town had been seeing this great, enormous UFO. That's why I started selling more UFO books, not because of my brilliant marketing."

Everyone but her, that is, had been seeing UFOs.

"Not only did I not see it," she said, "I didn't even hear about it at first."

An 1897 Airship Visit

But when she did start reading ongoing reports of sightings published in the *Empire-Tribune*, the local daily, Cannady did so with more than average knowledge of stellar objects. She had been an amateur astronomer for years. An avid reader since childhood, Cannady also is a student of science fiction, especially the pre-1900 speculative fiction that paved the way for later writers of futuristic fiction. She already knew, for example, that when it comes to UFOs, this rash of mysterious sightings was not Stephenville's first rodeo.

Moo-La the cow on the square in Stephenville

Cannady remembered having read that during the 1896-1897 wave of airship sightings from California to Texas, several Erath County residents said they had seen an aerial craft of some sort in their part of the world. Indeed, the Dallas *Morning News* reported on April 19, 1897, that Stephenville-area farmer C.L. McInhany, who lived on the Bosque River about three miles from town, claimed to have seen a cigar-shaped "aerial monster" about sixty feet in length.

"The motive power is an immense wheel at each end, in appearance much like a metallic windmill," the farmer told the Dallas newspaper. "It is driven by an immense electric engine, which derives its motive power from storage batteries."

Unlike the object that would be reported in Erath County more than 110 years later, the 1897 UFO was not airborne when McInhany saw it. Nor did it remain unidentified. Not only had it landed in his pasture, he got a chance to chat with the crew. The aviators gave their names as A. E. Dolbear and S.E. Tilman, he said. One was the pilot, the other served as engineer. The two men told McInhany they had taken the airship on a test flight for its New York inventors and had landed in Texas to make some minor repairs. "They are confident that they have achieved a great success and that within a short time navigation of the air will be an assured fact," McInhany said.

Though the Gay Nineties story of a Stephenville landing was doubtless just another fabricated newspaper piece in a multistate string of hoaxes and tongue-in-cheek "me, too" reports, whoever wrote the article can, all these years later, at least be credited with some impressive critical thinking for his day.

"[What do] you reckon is going to happen when dynamiters get to riding in airships and dropping bombs down on folks and cities? Is this world ready for airships?" the anonymous scribe quoted McInhany as having said.

The Wave Begins

Unlike bookseller Cannady, most Stephenville residents had no idea that their town had figured in a round of flying

226

object reports in the late 19th century. Near the end of the first decade of the 21st century, they went about trying to live up to their New Year's resolutions until suddenly finding themselves in the national spotlight.

Though some people later reported seeing something weird in the sky over Stephenville as early as November 2007, the sightings peaked eight days into the new year. Two days later, on January 10, 2008, the *Empire-Tribune* ran a page-one story by reporter Angela Joiner under a headline reading: "Four area residents witness mysterious objects, lights in Selden sky."

Steve Allen, a private pilot with more than thirty years experience, told Joiner he saw a giant set of flashing lights in the sky about 6:15 p.m. on January 8 in Selden. Allen ventured to the small community nine miles south of Stephenville to visit Mike and Claudette Odom, and all three witnessed the same thing. While they did not see an actual object, the lights appeared to be connected to one thing more than a mile long.

"We all flipped out," Allen said the next day. "I didn't sleep a wink last night."

What they saw appeared to be about 3,500 feet in the air and moving at a high rate of speed while making no sound. Flashing like strobes, the lights changed from a single horizontal line into a pair of vertical lines that appeared to be at least a quarter-mile apart. Then the lights morphed into what looked like white flames and vanished. Ten minutes later, as the men continued to discuss what in the world—or out of it— that they had seen, the lights reappeared.

"It wasn't a plane," said Claudette Odom, a former airline flight attendant. "I know how planes move. Honestly, I think it was a UFO. It was so fast you couldn't have put a finger on it and move it fast enough to follow it."

Joiner followed up her first report with another one the next day, January 11. "A number of area residents have come forward saying they also saw the mysterious lights witnessed by Steve Allen and friends…in Selden," she wrote.

One of the new witnesses was Lee Roy Gaitan, a constable from the Erath County community of Dublin.

"I was outside with my eight-year-old son," he said, "when I saw lights. It was like nothing I've ever seen before."

Gaitan called for his wife to come outside, and she saw the lights as well.

"I went to my pickup and got my binoculars to see if I could see a plane or something," he continued. "Even with the binoculars there was no outline. It started moving towards Stephenville and moving so fast I had trouble following it....It covered a big area."

When Fort Worth-based Associated Press reporter Angela K. Brown saw Joiner's stories, she interviewed Allen, Gaitan, and another man who said he had had seen a large metallic object. The wire service distributed her story worldwide.

Careful to keep her dispatch in perspective, Brown pointed out that roughly 200 UFO sightings per month in the United States get reported to private UFO-tracking groups like the Mutual UFO Network, better known by its acronym MUFON. Most of those reports, she noted, originate in California, Colorado, and Texas. She also cited an October 2007 poll conducted by AP and Ipsos, a French company specializing in survey-based research, in which 34 percent of the U.S. respondents said they believed in UFOs with 14 percent saying they had seen one.

Constable Gaitan told Brown he wasn't saying he had observed "a flying saucer." But, he continued, "it wasn't an airplane and I've never seen anything like it. I think it must be some kind of military craft—at least I hope it was."

But the AP story also quoted Major Karl Lewis, spokesman for the 301st Fighter Wing at the Joint Reserve Base Naval Air Station in Fort Worth, as saying that none of his wing's F-16s or any other aircraft from the military base (the former Carswell Air Force Base) had been in the air the night of January 8.

The January 15 publication of Brown's article set off a second round of "alien" sightings in Stephenville as mainstream and not-so-mainstream reporters, photographers, and television producers invaded the normally quiet town. "Moo-La," a black and white fiberglass dairy cow erected on the courthouse square in 1972 to tout Erath County's milk industry, became one of the most photographed objects in town. Though some religious fundamentalists in the area may have seen the outbreak of sightings as a sign that the Biblical end times had arrived, others with a more capitalistic bent viewed the phenomenon as a new cash cow.

A variety of Stephenville UFO T-shirts soon hit the local market, and the town's Chamber of Commerce saw a notable upswing in requests for tourism information. Despite the influx of reporters and ufologists, the owners of Jake and Dorothy's Café—a Stephenville landmark that has been in business since July 12, 1948—continued to observe "dollar a burger" night every Tuesday.

Some found humor in the sightings. One wag suggested space aliens had merely misread their cosmic map, mistaking "Erath" for "Earth." Someone else said the aliens may have only been hankering for a Dr. Pepper from the bottling plant in Dublin that still uses the soft drink's original, sugar-rich formula.

The publicity had already caught the eye of Kenneth Cherry, director of the Texas chapter of MUFON. Cherry decided the Stephenville sightings needed the further attention of his organization and set up a town meeting for January 19 to give locals a forum for relating their accounts.

A couple of hundred people showed up for the event.

"We believe there is some sort of phenomenon in action here," Cherry told the AP. "We see a pattern. But it will take months to investigate."

Cherry stressed that MUFON did not take the position that alien space craft actually exist. "All we are trying to do is figure out if we can explain it or not, and then we'll let the chips fall where they may."

Though the Air Force had initially said it had no aircraft in the vicinity of Stephenville on January 8, two weeks later the military reversed its stand. Declaring that it did so "in the interest of public awareness," the Air Force issued a statement that eight F-16 fighter jets had been training in the Stephenville area the night of the multiple UFO sightings. The jets entered one of six sectors comprising the Brownwood Military Operating Area, a 3,200-square mile area designated for military training flights, at 6:17 p.m. and left at 6:58 p.m. that Sunday. Minus the exact number of aircraft and the times, which were revealed later, the AP's Brown quickly ran with the story.

"So much for aliens in Texas dairy country," she wrote. But, she continued, "Some residents [who said they had seen the UFO] aren't buying it…saying the military's revelation actually bolsters their claims because several reported seeing at least two fighter jets chasing an object." In other words, some people believed that the only reason the F-16s had been in the vicinity of Stephenville was to investigate a UFO.

Brown talked to Stephenville fabric store owner Anne Frazor, who said that she and many others had seen military jets over Erath County but that what she saw on January 8 was something else. "I couldn't begin to say what it was," she told the AP staffer, "but to me it wasn't planes."

Back at the Bookstore

Regardless of what people saw or didn't see, bookstore owner Cannady realized a new chapter in Erath County history was unfolding. Someday, she knew, people would look back on the events of 2008 just as she and others had pondered the so-called Great Airship Mystery of 1896-1897.

With that in mind, she decided to host at meeting at her bookstore on January 24 to give people a second venue to discuss what had been going on and what they had seen. In addition to taking statements at the meeting that night, she said she would be happy to receive statements at any future time a witness wanted to come forth.

Eventually, Cannady collected more than thirty written or taped reports from area residents who said they had seen something unusual in or around Erath County. Though most of the reported sightings had occurred on January 8, sightings continued in the area.

At 6:05 a.m. on January 31, sixty-two-year-old Mike Zimmerman got up to go to the bathroom. Retired from the Texas Department of Public Safety, Zimmerman had spent twenty-five years with the state law enforcement agency, including nineteen years on the DPS' governor's protective detail. Walking back to bed that morning, Zimmerman happened to look out his bedroom window.

"I saw three bright lights," he later told Joiner. "Two white lights were grouped closer together and higher, and the third one was closer to the horizon. That one was a reddish orange color."

As Zimmerman continued to watch, he saw pulsating, strobe-like lights emitting from the two white lights. The third light remained static with no pulses.

The former state trooper, trained to be observant and to remember details, initially thought he was seeing three helicopters in operation. But he knew choppers would not have strobes as bright as the ones he was seeing. He found the lights so unusual he awakened his fiancé to look at them, but he waited a while before going public with what he had seen.

In mid-February, Joiner left the *Empire-Tribune*. Soon she put up a Web site (www.Stephenvillelights.com) and continued to post updates to the story she first broke in the Stephenville newspaper. Most of her Web articles reported new sightings, such as the one she posted about Zimmerman on February 28:

"Stephenville UFO is viewed by former protector of Texas Governors."

By March, most of the reporters and television crews had come and gone. Near the end of the month, Cannady hosted a couple of fellow bibliophiles from Fort Worth. At some point during their visit, Cannady offered to show her friends Stephenville's bat colony.

"We don't have as many bats as there are under the Congress Avenue Bridge in Austin," she said, "but we do have a nice little colony."

Grabbing a flashlight, Cannady led her friends from her bookstore to an alley off South Belknap Street, behind one of the row of buildings fronting the courthouse square.

"The gal and I were looking toward the top of the old stone building where the bats hang out," Cannady said. "Suddenly we saw something in the sky over the building and my friend says to her partner, 'Do you see what we see?' And he said, 'Yep, Mexican free-tail bats.' "

But Cannady and her friend were looking at something else.

"No," the Fort Worth woman said, "We mean that cigar-shaped thing."

Cannady and her fellow book dealers from Cow Town forgot about the bats and focused their attention on the object in the sky.

"My grandfather worked in the aerospace industry. He and I spent many an hour watching the skies for satellites and the like," Cannady said. "I've seen all sorts of 'lights in the sky,' both man-made and otherwise, and it was nothing like I've ever seen. I know it sounds like a cliché, but it was shaped like a cigar and had five or six lights on its side. It hung there in the sky for a minute and then zipped out of view behind one of the buildings."

Later, her friends, who requested anonymity, filled out a report for inclusion in the archive Cannady started.

Wayne Keeler, a private pilot who has spent 600 hours flying, also saw something in the sky at the end of March. In a hand-written statement dated March 31, 2008, Keeler wrote:

> About 8 p.m. two bright white lights appeared about 10 miles south of Stephenville as seen from near downtown. They had about the same general appearance as the plant Venus and were mistaken for stars until their movement to the east became apparent. [They] appeared to follow one after the other by about a mile and about 3 to 5 thousand feet of height. They proceeded to the east until out of sight. Their brightness was unvarying with no colored lights, such as aviation position and anti-collision lights....

The MUFON Report

MUFON released its report on the Stephenville sightings on July 10, 2008. Written by Glen Schulze and Robert Powell, the seventy-seven-page document attempted to collate witness reports (no names were used) with radar data. Ranging from plainly written to jargon-heavy at times, the report contained a series of computer-generated charts developed from analysis of radar images.

The eight investigators who had come to Stephenville had collected seventeen statements from witnesses who said they saw an unknown object between 6:00 and 9:30 p.m. on January 8. "This is a very large number of sightings to occur during only one day and within a four-hour period," the report said.

"Eight of these reports provided sufficient detail to identify a time and direction of the sighting of the object. Witnesses in these reports included a constable, a chief of police, a private pilot, and a former air traffic control operator."

While MUFON has no shortage of UFO sightings to log in any given year, the Stephenville sighting was unusual in that the organization had been able to obtain radar data through a federal Freedom of Information Act request that "indicates unidentified aircraft without transponder beacons which...were found in the same compass direction and time frame as citied by witnesses [of the UFO.]"

"As to what these witnesses saw," the report concluded, "it is difficult to determine. It was not any known aircraft. The enormous size of the object, its complete silence, and its ability to travel at high rates of speed and also to remain stationary or travel at slow speeds, is not explained by any known aircraft."

Not only that, the object had been on a track toward then-President George W. Bush's ranch at Crawford, seventy-three miles southeast of Stephenville. While that aspect of the report made for lively speculation, the media, particularly Joiner in her Web site assessment of the document, found the report long on verbiage but short on substance. One thing the report did not do was stop reports of things in the sky over Erath County.

As fall settled over North Texas in October 2008, yet another round of sightings occurred in and around Stephenville. This short-lived wave did not draw another MUFON investigative team, but it once again made headlines.

"Recent accounts started coming in Tuesday, Oct. 21," the *Empire-Tribune* reported. "More sightings were reported Wednesday night [October 22] and a stadium full of parents watching a Junior High football game spotted more strange lights Thursday night."

Using his mother's digital camera, one student shot thirty seconds of video of the oval-shaped object he saw, his footage airing on Dallas and Houston television stations on October 24. Both his parents also viewed the object.

"It was a round thing," the student's mother told a reporter with Dallas' WFAA. "You could see lights around it, flickering and changing. It was awesome."

The broadcast journalist also interviewed *Empire-Tribune* reporter Whitney Ashley who said several employees of the newspaper and other Erath County residents had seen the object but did not want to have their names used. But another ten witnesses, she said, had no problem with going on the record about what they had seen.

Another Dallas reporter, long-time history columnist Kent Biffle—a veteran journalist who had taken to the skies in a small plane to chase UFOs over Dallas-Fort Worth in August 1965—thought to contact a former Air Force officer who had been involved in the long-closed Project Blue Book effort.

Retired officer Bob Callahan told Biffle he had left he project thinking that extraterrestrial visits are "possible." Looking back on his role in the Air Force's last official effort to investigate unidentified flying objects, he said: "We were able to explain approximately 90 percent of what we investigated. The rest, we reported out as 'unexplainable' or needing additional information before a final report could be issued."

A year after the Stephenville sightings, another investigator concluded that the lights so many people had seen could indeed be explained.

Noting that the July 2008 MUFON investigative product had caused "much mischief," the editors of *Skeptical Inquirer*, the publication of the Committee for Skeptical Inquiry, offered a far different slant on the Stephenville sightings in their January-February 2009 edition. In an article titled "The Stephenville Lights: What Actually Happened," the editors said that retired Air Force officer James McGaha, director of Grasslands Observatory at Tucson, Arizona, had analyzed the

MUFON report. The astronomer had concluded that while the radar data acquired by the organization contained 2.5 million "points of noise and scatter" MUFON had "selected just 187 of these points to contend that radar had tracked a huge 'object'...traveling near the Western White House...." McGaha said that amounted to "cherry picking...." He added, "This analysis is absurd."

What people had actually seen over Erath County that night, McGaha continued, were F-16 fighters dropping LUU/2B/B flares—parachuted devices that create an intense light that burns for four minutes with 2 million candlepower—while engaging in night maneuvers. Even at a distance of 150 miles, he said, such a flare would appear to be as bright as the planet Venus.

"The F-16s did not react to any unknown targets," McGaha concluded, "and radar did not detect any unknown targets...Nothing otherworldly happened around Stephenville on January 8, 2008."

And while that seems to be the end of the story, many who saw the lights above Stephenville would say it's not. They are absolutely convinced that what they saw was not from this world as much as those who say it was man-made. Who's right? Perhaps we'll never know. Or maybe someday we will.

BIBLIOGRAPHY

General Sources

Ball, Danny. Interviews with author by phone and e-mail, September 2008.

Brookesmith, Peter. *UFO: The Government Files.* London: Brown Packaging Ltd., 1996.

Condon, Dr. Edward U; Gillmore, Daniel S., editor; et al.; *Scientific Study of Unidentified Flying Objects.* New York: E.P. Dutton & Co., Inc., in association with Colorado Associated University Press, 1969.

Haines, Gerald K. "CIA's Role in the Study of UFOs, 1947-90." *Studies in Intelligence*, Vol. 1, No. 1, 1997.

Hynek, J. Allen. *The Hynek UFO Report.* New York: Barnes & Noble Books, 1997 (originally published in 1977).

_____. *The UFO Experience: A Scientific Inquiry.* New York: Ballantine Books, 1972.

Keyhoe, Donald E. *Flying Saucers from Outer Space.* New York: Henry Holt and Company, 1953.

_____. and Gordon I. R. Lore, Jr., editors. *UFOs: A New Look, A Special Report by the National Investigations Committee on Aerial Phenomena.* Washington, D.C.: NICAP, 1969.

Randles, Jenny, and Hough, Peter. *The Complete Book of UFOs.* New York: Sterling Publishing Co., Inc. 1996.

Ruppelt, Edward J. *The Report on Unidentified Flying Objects.* New York, Ace Books, 1956.

Steiger, Brad (editor). *Project Blue Book: Top Secret UFO Findings Revealed.* New York: Ballantine Books, 1976.

Treat, Wesley; Shade, Heather; Riggs, Rob. *Weird Texas.* New York: Sterling Publishing Co., Inc. 2005.

Chapter 1: In the Beginning: Texas' Earliest UFOs

Dallas *Morning News*, selected issues.

Denison *News*, January 25, 1878.

Dublin *Progress*, June 17, 1891.

New York *Times*, July 6, 1873.

Chapter 2: Death from Outer Space: Or Joe Mulhatton Strikes Again

Burlington, Iowa *Weekly Hawkeye*, April 26, 1883.

Branch, Walter. "Chronological Listing of Meteorites That Have Struck Man-Made Objects, Humans and Animals." www.branchmeteorites.com/metstruck.html

Galveston *Daily News*, selected issues.

"Joseph Mulhattan [sic]." www.museumofhoaxes.com/hoax/Hoaxipedia/Joseph_Mul hattan.html

McNamee, Gregory. "Arizona's Tallest Tale-Teller." www.desertusa.com/mag98/april/stories/tale.html

Newport, Rhode Island, *Daily News*, April 16, 1883.

"The Original Joe Mulhatton Talks." Galveston *Daily News*, July 15, 1890.

Stowers, Carlton. "A Quest For Preservation." *Texas Parks & Wildlife*, November 1999.

Thomas, Sidney J. *Scrapbook.* NP, nd.

"Wanderer in the Skies." New York *Times*, January 30, 1883.

"When the Sky Fell in Texas." www.utexas.edu/features/2005/odessa/index.html

Chapter 3: Judge Proctor's Windmill

Charitan, Wallace O. *The Great Texas Airship Mystery*. Plano: Wordware Publishing, 1991.

Bailey, Brad. "Imaginative minds keep alive 1897 legend of spaceman's run-in with Aurora windmill." Dallas *Morning News*, April 17, 1983.

Beach, Patrick. "When it comes to UFO's, Texas has plenty of true believers deep in their hearts." Austin *American-Statesman*, July 27, 1997.

Dallas *Morning News*, April 18, 1897, and selected other issues.

Dallas *Times-Herald*, selected issues.

Flemmons, Jerry. "Once Upon a Time in Aurora." *Southern Living*, February 1971.

Learner, Preston. "Aurora revisited." Fort Worth *Star-Telegram*, March 31, 1986.

Mutual UFO Network. Aurora, Texas case file. www.mufon.com

Pegues, Etta. *Aurora, Texas: The Town That Might Have Been*. Newark, Texas: Privately published, 1975.

Peralta, Eyder. "The Aurora mystery." Fort Worth *Star-Telegram*, February 28, 2007.

Porterfield, Billy. "The Aurora Spaceman." *Texas Observer*, September 21, 1973.

Porterfield, Billy. Interview with author, Wimberley, Texas, October 16, 2008.

Stowers, Carlton. "Heavenly Hoax: Texas town has its own brush with a UFO." Dallas *Observer*, April 3, 2003.

Tolbert, Frank X. "Did Plane Crash in Texas in 1897?" Dallas *Morning News*, January 4, 1967.

Chapter 4: Bright Lights, Big Mysteries

Abernethy, Francis E. *Tales from the Big Thicket*. Austin: University of Texas Press, 1966.

Alpine *Avalanche*, selected issues.

Ansley, Kevin. Interview with author via e-mail, June 2008.

Bunnell, James. Interview with author via e-mail, June 2008.

_____. *Night Orbs*. Cedar Creek, Texas: Lacey Publishing Company, 2003.

Brueske, Judith M., Ph.D. *The Marfa Lights: Being a Collection of First-Hand Accounts by People Who Have Seen the Lights Close-Up or in Unusual Circumstances, and Related Material*. Alpine, Texas: Ocotillo Enterprises, 1988.

Cox, Mike. *Stand-Off in Texas: "Just Call Me a Spokesman for DPS..."* Austin, Texas: Eakin Press, 1998.

Dallas *Morning News*, selected issues.

Devereux, Paul, with Clarke, David; Roberts, Andy; and McCartney, Paul. *Earth Lights Revelation*. London, Blanford Press, 1989 and 1990.

Foreman, Jim. "The Dancing Ghosts of the Chinatis." *Grain Producers News*, August 1979.

Graham, Douglas D. "The Marfa Lights." *Texas Parks & Wildlife*, January 1999.

Handbook of Texas Online, http://www.tshaonline.org/handbook/online/articles/AA/hga4.html

Homan, Bryant "Eduardo." The "Marfa Lights" of Mexico, Book excerpt reprinted in *The Desert Candle*, Vol. 10, No. 4, July-August 1996.

Houston *Chronicle*, selected issues.

"Marfa Lights," leaflet prepared by the Museum of the Big Bend, Sul Ross State University, Alpine, Texas: undated.

Miles, Elton. *More Tales of the Big Bend*. Texas A&M University Press, 1988.

Munson, Catherine Foster. *Ghosts along the Brazos*. Waco: Texian Press, 1977.

Pecos *Enterprise*, selected issues.

Real Haunted Houses Web site, http://www.realhaunts.com/united-states/texas/anson/shine-your-lantern/

Southwest Ghost Hunters Association Web site, http://www.sgha.net/tx/anson/anson2.html.

Riggs, Rob. *In the Big Thicket: On the Trail of the Wild Man*. New York: Paraview Press, 2001.

San Angelo *Standard-Times*, selected issues.

San Antonio *Express*, selected issues.

Wikipedia:
http://en.wikipedia.org/wiki/Anson%2C_Texas,
http://en.wikipedia.org/wiki/Clayton_Williams,
http://en.wikipedia.org/wiki/St._Elmo's_fire
http://en.wikipedia.org/wiki/Ball_lightning
http://en.wikipedia.org/wiki/Stephen_F._Austin

Williams, Rosemary. "The Marfa Lights: A Mystery." *Texas Highways*, August 1993.

Chapter 5: The Roswell Incident—A UFO Legend from Outer Texas, 1947

Albuquerque *Journal*, selected editions.

Ashcroft, Bruce. Interview with author by telephone, April 1999.

Associated Press. " 'Saucer Man' Doubts Disks Exist; Says Air Force Finds No Basis." New York *Times*, August 4, 1952.

Booth, William. "At Roswell Festival, Doubt is an Alien Concept." Washington *Post*, July 8, 2008.

Berkowitz, Lana. "You're never alone in Roswell." Houston *Chronicle*, July 26, 2005.

http://www.aztecufo.com

Davis, Richard. "Government Records: Results of a Search for Records Concerning the 1947 Crash near Roswell, New Mexico," a letter to Congressman Steven H. Schiff dated July 28, 1995. *SIRS Government Reporter*, spring 1999.

Distinguished Service Cross citation for Roger M. Ramey. www.homeofheroes.com/valor/1_Citations/03_wwii-dsc/aaf_p.html

Foley, Bill. "Flying saucer craze climaxed in 1947." *Florida Times Union*, July 11, 1997.

Green, Sherri Deatherage. "UFO euphoria invades Roswell for 52 years." *PRWeek* U.S. edition, May 7, 1999.

Haut, Walter. Interview with author by telephone, April 1999.

International UFO Museum and Research Center Web site, www.ifumrc.com.

Klass, Philip J. "Key Roswell 'eyewitness' changes story significantly." CSICOP's Online Archive of The Skeptics UFO Newsletter (SUN): #31, January 1995, www.csicop.org/klassfiles/SUN-31.html

McAndrew, Capt. James. *The Roswell Report: Case Closed.* Washington, D.C.: Headquarters United States Air Force, 1997.

Mayfield, Elaine. Interview with author by telephone, March 18, 2008.

Roswell *Record*, selected editions.

Suid, Lawrence. "Lights! Camera! NASA!" *Space World*, June 1987.

Schmitt, Donald R., and Carey, Thomas J. "Roswell: 52 Years of Unanswered Questions." The J. Allen Hynek Center for UFO Studies Web site. http://www.cufos.org/ros6.html

Thomas, Dave. "The Roswell Incident and Project Mogul." *The Skeptical Inquirer*, Vol. 19, No. 1, January/February 1995.

Weaver, Col. Richard L., and McAndrew, 1st Lt. James. "The Roswell Report: Fact vs. Fiction in the New Mexico

Desert," executive summary. Washington, D.C.: Headquarters United States Air Force, 1995.

Chapter 6: Attack on Camp Hood

"1949-Fort Hood UFO Wave." UFO Casebook Files. www.ufocasebook.com/fthood1949.html
"Brief history of Killeen Base; now West Fort Hood." www.pao.hood.army.mil/history/1950s/a_brief_history_of_killeen_base.html
"Nuclear Chronology." Office of the Deputy Assistant to the Secretary of Defense for Nuclear Matters www.acq.osd.mil/ncbdp/nm/nuclearchronology1.html
"UFO Sighting Report August 2nd 2007: Killeen Ft. Hood, Texas, USA." www.ufoinfo.com/sightings/usa/070802.shtml
"Weapons of Mass Destruction (WMD)." www.globalsecurity.org/wmd/facility/q_area-intro.html

Chapter 7: "Damn…Look at Those Lights!"

Davis, Kenneth. Interview with author, Canyon, Texas, April 5, 2008.
Lubbock *Avalance-Journal*, selected issues.
Story, Ronald D. *The Encyclopedia of UFOs.* Garden City, New York: Dolphin Books, 1980.
"There Is A Case For Interplanetary Saucers." *Life,* April 7, 1952.
Wheeler, David R. *The Lubbock Lights.* New York: Award Books, 1977.

Chapter 8: Military Pilots Saw Them, Too—Laredo and Galveston: 1952

Air Force Magazine, selected issues.

Galveston *Daily News,* selected issues.

Gordon, John Steele. "Ivy Mike and the Ultimate Bomb." www.AmericanHeritage.com, posted January 18, 2008.

Houston *Chronicle*, selected issues.

Houston *Post*, selected issues.

Jung, C.G., translated by R.E. C. Hull. *Flying Saucers: A Modern Myth of Things Seen in the Skies.* New York: Princeton University Press, 1978

Keyhoe, Donald E. *Flying Saucers from Outer Space.* New York: Henry Holt and Company, 1953.

http://www.blueblookarchive.org

http://www.globalsecurity.org/military/facility/ellington.htm

http://nicap.org/texas/fogledoc1.htm

http://nicap.org/texas/fogledoc2.htm

http://nicap.org/texas/fogledoc3.htm

http://nicap.org/texas/fogledoc4.htm

http://www.nicap.org/texas/fogledoc9.htm

http://www.nicap.org/texas/fogledoc10.htm

http://www.ufodna.com/uf12/uf7/127626.htm

http://en.wikipedia.org/wiki/Donald_Keyhoe

http://en.wikipedia.org/wiki/Ground_Observer_Corps

New York *Times,* selected issues.

UFO Casebook.
http://www.ufocasebook.com/1952b29galveston.html and http://www.ufocasebook.com/gulfmexico.html

Chapter 9: Keeping Secrets: A 1950s Pastime

http://americanairlinesstewardess.blogspot.com

"Fail to Identify Near-Crash Plane." El Paso *Herald-Post*, July 18, 1957.

Klass, Phillipp. *UFOs Explained.* New York: Random House, 1974.

McDonald, James. "Twenty-two Years of Inadequate UFO Investigations." Paper delivered at American Association for the Advancement of Science, 134th Meeting, General Symposium, Unidentified Flying Objects, Tucson, Arizona, Dec. 27, 1969.

"Miss USA Exposed As Wife, Mother." Corpus Christi *Caller-Times*, July 19, 1957.

"Mystery Ship Near Crash Was Airliner." El Paso *Herald-Post*, Aug. 2, 1957.

Project Blue Book case file No. 10073, Files of 1957, National Archives and Record Administration, Washington, D.C.

"The RB-47 radar visual multiple witnesses cases, July 17, 1957." http://www.ufologie.net/htm/rb47.htm

"RB-47 Specifications." http://www.globalsecurity.org/intell/systems/rb-47-specs.htm

"Semi-Finalist Vie in Beauty Contest," Galveston *Daily News*, July 18, 1957.

Sparks, Brad. "RB-47 Radar/Visual Case," in Jerome Clark (ed.), *The UFO Enclyclopedia*, 2nd. ed., Detroit: Omnigraphics, 1998, Vol. 2, pp. 761b-790b.

http://ivegotasecretonline.com
http://www.nicap.org/rb47_update_sparks.htm
http://www.ufocasebook.com/rb47.html

Chapter 10: Levelland's "Fiery Object" Stopped Cars

Abilene *Reporter-News*, selected issues.

Burleson, Donald R. "Levelland, Texas, 1957: Case Reopened." *International UFO* Journal, Vol. 28, Spring 2004.

Lubbock *Avalanche-Journal*, selected issues.

Rullan, Antonio F. "The Southwestern Wave of 1957," *International UFO Reporter*, Vol. 31, No. 3, 2007.

Wheeler, David R. *The Lubbock Lights*. New York: Award Books, 1977.

Chapter 11: A Texas UFO Factory—Columbia Scientific Balloon Facility

Albuquerque *Journal*, selected issues.

Associated Press, selected articles.

Browne, Malcolm W. "Balloon Bargains Lure Scientists." New York *Times*. October 1, 1985.

www.nsbf.nasa.gov

Stipp, David. "Scientific Research Is Ballooning Today In Palestine, Texas." *Wall Street Journal*. October 20, 1983.

"Testing device drops in on startled family." St. Petersburg *Times*. October 15, 1987.

Chapter 12: The Skies over Sherman—1898 and 1965

Dallas *Morning News*, selected issues.

Denton *Record-Chronicle*, selected issues.

Lorenzen, Coral E. *Flying Saucers: The Startling Evidence of the Invasion from Outer Space*. New York and Toronto: Signet Books, 1966.

Edwards, Frank. *Flying Saucers—Serious Business*. New York: Bantam Books, 1966.

New York *Times*, selected issues.

Sherman *Democrat*, selected issues.

Sherman *Democrat-Herald*, selected issues.

Sherman *Register*, selected issues.

www.ufocasebook.com/shermantexas1965.html

Wilkins, Harold T. *Flying Saucers on the Attack*. New York: Ace Books Inc, 1954 (reprinted with additional material in 1967).

www.cohenufo.org/nwswk_66_hynek.html

Chapter 13: Friday Night Lights—Damon, Texas: September 3, 1965

Angelton *Times*, selected issues.

Brazosport *Facts*, selected issues.

Fuller, G. *Incident at Exeter*. New York: G.P. Putnam's—Berkley Medallion Edition, 1966.

Griffin, Andrew. "Avoyelles Parish Man's Disappearance Still a Mystery after 50 years." *The Town Talk*. Alexandria, Louisiana. July 20, 2003.

McCoy, Billy. Interview with author, December 6, 2008.

McCoy, Billy. Oral history transcript of interview conducted by Colleen Kenyon, July 17, 1985.

http://www.ufocasebook.com/damontexas.html

http://www.mysterious-america.net/updateonf-89jeti.html

http://www.ufocasebook.com/kinrossupdate.html

http://ufos.about.com/od/bestufocasefiles/p/exeter.htm

Chapter 14: Close Encounter of the East Texas Kind—Huffman, Texas, 1980

"Burns Follow UFO Incident." *The APRO Bulletin*," Vol. 29, No. 8, 1981, pp 1-4.

Death certificate records. County Clerk's Office, Montgomery County, Texas.

Donovan, Dick. "Three live in pain and terror after attack by blazing UFO." *Weekly World News*, March 21, 1981.

Houston *Chronicle*, selected issues.

Houston *Post*, selected issues.

Schuessler, John. *The Cash-Landrum UFO Incident.* La Porte, Texas: GeoGraphics Printing Co., 1998.

_____. "The Texas UFO Trauma." *UFO Report*, nd. http://en.wikipedia.org/wiki/Cash-Landrum_incident

Obituaries. *Big Thicket Messenger*, September 23, 2007. Accessed at http://www.easttexasnews.com/Obituaries/Obituaries_Mess enger/September2007/september23_2007.html.

http://www.ufocasebook.com/Pineywoods.html. "The Pineywoods Incident, Cash-Landrum."

Sparks, Brad. "Cash-Landrum: NOT Ionizing Radiation," December 30, 1998. Accessed at http://www.qtm.net/~geibdan/a1999/cash3.htm.

"Transcript of Bergstrom AFB Interview of Betty Cash, Vickie & Colby Landrum," Parts 1 and 2, August 17, 1981. http://www.cufon.org/cufon/cashlani.htm and http://www.cufon.org/cufon.cashlani2.htm.

Chapter 15: UFO Lore Crashes and Burns on the Border

Acheson, Dean. *Present at the Creation: My Years in the State Department.* New York: W.W. Norton &. Co., 1969. http://www.ufoevidence.org/cases/case378.htm http://www.ufoevidence.org/Cases/CaseSubarticle.asp?ID=379

Isaacson, Walter, and Thomas, Evan. *The Wise Men.* New York: Simon and Shuster, 1986.

Ragsdale, Kenneth Baxter. *Wings over the Mexican Border: Pioneer Military Aviation in the Big Bend.* Austin, Texas: University of Texas Press, 1984.

Randel, Kevin. Case MJ-12: *The True Story Behind the Government's UFO Conspiracies.* New York: HARPERTORCH, 2002.

Steinman, Williams W. *UFO Crash at Aztec.* Tucson: Privately published by Wendelle Stevens, 1986. http://en.wikipedia.org/wiki/Majestic_12

Torres, Noe, and Uriarte, Ruben. *Mexico's Roswell: The Chihuahua UFO Crash.* College Station, Texas: Virtualbookworm.com, 2007.

Truman, Harry S. *Memoirs of Harry S. Truman: Volume Two: 1-46-52, Years of Trial and Hope.* New York: Doubleday, 1955-1956.
http://home.pacbell.net/hoerit/docs2/crash/crshlist.htm
http://www.texfiles.com/ufo/UFOBBS/2000/2835.ufo
http://www.nicap.org/reports/rina4.htm

Chapter 16: A Cow Country Classic: Bovina 1995

The Handbook of Texas Online,
http://www.tshaonline.org/handbook/online/articles/BB/hjb13.html
Haulman, Daniel L. U.S. Air Force Fact Sheet, 27 Fighter Wing (ACC).
Texas Escapes Online:
http://www.texasescapes.com/TexasPanhandleTowns/Bovina-Texas.htm
UFO Evidence.org,
http://www.ufoevidence.org/cases/case225.htm
Webb, Walter N. *Final Report on the America West Airline Case, May 25-26, 1995.* Chicago: The UFO Research Coalition, 1996.
West Texas Sky Wonders:
http://community-2.webtv.net/nikcole/westtexasskywonders2/
Wikipedia, http://en.wikipedia.org/wiki/Bovina,_Texas and http://en.wikipedia.org/wiki/Sightings

Chapter 17: Stephenville Lights: "We all flipped out."

Biffle, Kent. "Stephenville area's had its share of UFO sightings." Dallas *Morning News*, February 4, 2008.

Brown, Angela K. "Dozens in Texas town report seeing UFO." Associated Press, January 15, 2008.

_____. "Military now says planes flying in area of UFO reports." Associated Press, January 23, 2008.

Cannady, Sarah. Interview with author, Stephenville, Texas, October 21, 2008.

Frazier, Matt. "UFO investigators land in Dublin to quiz locals." Fort Worth *Star-Telegram*, January 20, 2008.

"Group takes UFO sightings statements." Associated Press, January 20, 2008.

Hammons, Steve. "Interpreting the MUFON Stephenville UFO radar report: What does it say?" www.ufodigest.com/news/0708/mufon-stephenville.html

Joiner, Angela. Stephenville *Empire-Tribune*, selected issues.

_____. "Stephenville UFO report out." Abilene *Reporter-News*, June 14, 2008.

Marrs, Jim. "There's Something Weird Going on in Stephenville, Texas Right Now." *UFO Magazine*, Vol. 23, No. 2, March 2008.

"More lights spotted in Stephenville skies." Stephenville *Empire-Tribune*, October 24, 2008.

Morgan, Jerry. "UFO Hunters and Sighters Swarm Dublin Meeting." De Leon *Free Press*, January 24, 2008.

Mutual UFO Network. "Special Research Report, Stephenville, Texas." Fort Collins, Colorado, 2008.

www.stephenvillelights.com

"The Stephenville Lights: What Actually Happened," *Skeptical Inquirer*, January-February, 2009.

LaVergne, TN USA
21 September 2010
197871LV00002B/1/P